# Hollywood's Babe

## Dancing Through Oz

*For Sandy!*

*Enjoy!*

*Love,*

*Caren Marsh-Doll*

# Hollywood's Babe

## Dancing Through Oz

An Autobiography
by Caren Marsh-Doll

For my son, Jonathan, with love

## Special thanks to:

Mike Eves
Louise Marsh
Bill Marx
Dorothy Morris
Bruce Page
Deane Pearcy
Joyce Spizer
William Stillman
Jamie Workman

## and a very special thanks to:

Robert Van Aken
and
Josh Curtis

Published in the USA by:
BearManor Media
P O Box 71426
Albany, Georgia 31708
www.bearmanormedia.com

ISBN 1-59393-107-7

Printed in the United States of America.

Book & Cover design by Darlene & Dan Swanson of Van-garde Imagery, Inc.
All photos from the private collection of the author.

# Contents:

Let them praise His
name in the dance.

Psalms 149:3

# Prologue

I stood in front of Judy Garland's home. Not the small farmhouse in Kansas where she lived with Aunt Em and Uncle Henry. This two-story wood-frame house in Grand Rapids, Minnesota had once been where Judy lived with her parents, Ethel and Frank Gumm, and her two older sisters, Jimmie and Sue, and had been Judy's home until she reached the age of four. The home is now a museum.

A large sign with the words JUDY GARLAND'S BIRTH-PLACE stood at the curb to my left. A few yards away to my right were life-sized cutout figures of Dorothy, the Scarecrow, the Tin Woodsman, and the Cowardly Lion. Holes replaced faces, so visitors could stand behind a figure, with their faces in the holes, and have their pictures taken. On the walkway leading to the front door, paintings of yellow bricks scattered here and there boasted names, dates, and visitors' hometowns.

On this three-day festival in June 2001, I had been invited to attend as a celebrity guest on what would have been Judy's 79th birthday. Why me? Because, once upon a time, I was chosen to be Judy Garland's stand-in for that timeless movie, *The Wizard of Oz*. Other celebrity guests had included June Allyson, Mickey Rooney and his wife Jan, Margaret O'Brien, and Donald O'Conner.

When I entered the museum, I faced the living room with a staircase to the right, and in the corner a baby-grand piano and a Victrola. Floor-length white curtains graced the windows. In the kitchen, I recognized the stove as the same kind I'd seen in our home when I was a child. On the side porch stood a laundry tub with a wringer attached. My mother had washed clothes in a tub like that and let me turn the handle on the wringer before hanging the garments on the backyard line to dry.

Upstairs, an old-fashioned bathtub with four cast-iron feet and a small bedroom with two single beds, one against each wall for Judy's sisters, filled one side of the second story. Their bureau top held a curling iron and other items that young girls would have used in the 1920s. Down the hall at the front of the house was a larger bedroom with a double bed where her parents had slept. In a corner was a crib for little Frances—as she was then called—or, more affectionately, simply "Baby." I stood there looking at the crib. Who would have guessed then that that little tot would bring the whole world such joy with her voice and acting ability, especially in her role as Dorothy Gale in *The Wizard of Oz*?

On Friday evening, I spoke about my memories of working with Judy and my dance career. Saturday morning I taught a large group of people of all ages how to line dance. I included teaching them how to do the skipping step down the yellow brick road to the song "We're Off to See the Wizard." Saturday night they held a silent auction and presented the first Judy Garland Scholarship for Achievements in the Arts to a young lady. Richard Glazier, pianist and narrator, entertained us later with his fabulous show. Although the festival was an unforgettable experience, there was one very special moment that stirred in me a multitude of old memories. It caused me to reflect on my childhood desire, and the ultimate fulfillment of that desire.

On that final afternoon, a young woman with a bright-eyed little girl approached me. "I enjoyed your talk last evening," the woman said, "hearing about your *Wizard of Oz* experience and your movie and dancing career. Tell me, do you think my daughter is old enough to start dance lessons? She's only four, but every time she hears music she's so happy, moving and twirling to the melody. What would you suggest?"

The child looked up at me, anticipating my answer.

"How would you like to take dance lessons?" I asked.

Without any hesitation, her big brown eyes focused on mine as she replied, "That'd be cool."

In that moment, I flashed back to a time when I was four. I told her mother, "Get her started in a ballet class now. She's ready."

## Chapter One: 1923

"How would you like to take dance lessons?" my mother asked me as we walked past a dance studio a few blocks from our home in Hollywood, California. We passed the studio every time we went to the corner grocery store. I had seen little girls carrying their pretty pink slippers by their ribbons as they entered the studio with their mothers.

Mother continued, "You're four years old now, and I think it's important for a little girl to take dance lessons so she'll learn to be graceful in her walk and movements. Would you like that?"

"Yes, yes," I answered, "if I could wear those pretty pink slippers." I didn't know then that she had already inquired about the classes and had purchased ballet slippers for me.

My first lesson was on a Saturday afternoon. Dorothy, my one-year-old sister, stayed home with Daddy while Mother and I headed for the studio. I skipped beside her and swung my ballet shoes by their ribbons like I'd seen those other girls do.

I didn't know how much I'd like dance class. I did know it was always fun moving my little body to the music at home. And I liked to jump rope to the songs we'd sing and play ring-around-the-rosy to a simple little tune we all knew. It all seemed so natural.

When we arrived at the studio, other little girls and their mothers entered with us. We were all greeted by Doris Russell, the pretty dance teacher. I looked around the room not knowing what to expect. I remember the shiny wood floor. Mothers were seated along one wall to watch their daughters' first ballet class. One completely mirrored wall faced a long pole that extended parallel across another wall about as high as my shoulder. I wondered what that was for.

Some of the girls put their slippers on. I sat on the floor beside them and put mine on too. We all dressed differently. I wore my favorite pink cotton dress to match my slippers.

Miss Russell clapped her hands together and called, "All right, girls, everyone on the floor. Let's start."

There must have been at least fifteen of us pouring out onto the hardwood surface. Then she announced with a big smile, "This is a beginning ballet class. You're all new here, and we're going to have a wonderful time learning how to dance."

Miss Russell put us in a line that stretched across the room and asked what our names were as she approached each one of us. I liked her and was glad to be there. One little girl ran out of the line crying to her mother. I looked at Miss Russell, but she didn't seem to mind. I guess she'd seen girls do that before.

"Now," she said, "we will learn the five arm positions of the ballet."

She stood in front of us and proceeded to show—and tell us— what they were.

"First position," she said, demonstrating what we were to do, "arms forming a circle in front of our bodies." We all proceeded to imitate her.

"Second position. Arms out to each side."

We followed her movements.

"Third position. Right arm curved in front of your body. Left arm remains out to the side."

I watched her closely, wanting to do it just right.

"Fourth position. Left arm curved above the head."

Fifteen little girls; some tried to determine their left arm from their right.

"Fifth position. Bring your right arm up and curved to meet the left above your head."

Pleased with my circle, I looked around at the other girls to see how they were doing.

Our patient teacher put a record on the phonograph. I recognized "Blue Danube" because we played it at home. I looked at Mother and smiled. Then, in time to the music, Miss Russell called out, "First position. Second position. Third position. Fourth position. Fifth position—and hold it."

As I moved my arms in time to the music, I kept thinking, when are we going to dance?

She told us to take a five minute rest, and then we'd learn the five feet positions. I walked to Mother's chair. She smiled.

"Are you enjoying this?" she asked. "You did very well. Would you like to continue?"

"Oh yes," I said. "Am I graceful yet? When do we dance?"

"You are," she laughed. "And you will dance. You're learning the basics now." Little did I know then how many basic dance steps I would learn in the future.

Miss Russell called us back to the floor and told us to stand at the barre, as she pointed to that long pole. She told us to face it and hold on with both hands so we could learn the basic foot positions. At the end of the hour, I knew if what I'd learned so far were the basics, I couldn't wait to discover what was yet to come. Mother signed me up for a course of lessons while I removed my ballet slippers. On the walk home I couldn't stop talking about the class and Miss Russell, and all the little girls, and how much I loved wearing my pretty pink ballet shoes.

I practiced my basic positions at home and held on to the back of a chair as I would the barre. Sometimes I stayed a few minutes after class to watch the next, more advanced, dancers. They were older—probably ten or twelve, and they wore toe shoes, not ballet slippers. That's what I wanted to do—dance on my toes.

Many months later, Miss Russell granted my wish when she told Mother I was ready for toe shoes. It was so exciting, buying my first pair. The lady at the dance shop showed me how to stuff the toes of the shoes with lambs wool to protect my toes from blisters. I discovered later that no matter how well you stuffed them you could still get blisters, and sometimes, bloody toes. That was all part of being a toe dancer.

More months passed, and I loved my lessons. When I was five years old, Miss Russell announced to the class one day that she was going to have a studio recital for our parents and friends. I was surprised and excited when she told me I would perform the solo, "Glow Worm."

I practiced making my entrance to the strains of "Glow Little Glow Worm, glimmer, glimmer," stepped forward on my right toe, then the left, then up on both toes, and traveled to the center of the floor in tiny steps where I continued to dance. Oh, how I loved the feeling of moving to the music. Nothing could be more thrilling, I thought. I was so happy and felt in complete control of my little five-year-old body. I had never experienced such freedom, and I burst with joy. I felt I "glimmered" like that little Glow Worm. Then the record ended and so did my dance. Miss Russell told me it was an excellent performance and rewarded me with a big hug.

Mother took me to a shop my teacher had recommended where I could get my recital costume. We chose a pretty pink ballet outfit. Snug through the bodice, it burst out into a short tutu made of pink tulle. The shoulder straps, fashioned of pink roses, matched the three plump pink roses on the front of the waistline. A hair-band of pink roses set off my Dutch-bobbed hair. I felt beautiful and couldn't wait to dance at the recital to be held on a Saturday afternoon.

Two-year-old Dorothy sat on Daddy's lap while he and Mother watched the recital. Both sides of the studio filled with parents and friends who waited to see their children perform.

Miss Russell greeted everyone, announced that we were the youngest of all her classes, and that she was proud of every one of us. She walked over to the Victrola in the corner, wound it up, and started the music for the ten girls in the opening number. Their performance ended with robust applause.

The various dances continued, then as one group prepared to go offstage, Miss Russell, with her hand poised over the Victrola, signaled that I was next. My heart pounded so hard I thought everyone in the studio could hear it. Terrified, I felt it in my throat, throbbing so hard I thought it would leap out of my mouth. I wanted to run away. I glanced at my parents who watched the other dancers finish their number, and I wanted to cry out, "I don't want to do this!" I felt like I was going to throw up right there in front of everybody.

As the dancers left the floor and my music started, I could hear, "Glow Little Glow Worm," and my fear melted away. I stepped forward on my toes with assurance, danced through the number with confidence and regretted the moment the music ended. I was ecstatic! As I curtsied to the audience, I became aware of the applause and reveled in it.

When the recital ended, I flew over to Mother and Daddy and announced, "I'm not going to be a dancer - I *am* a dancer!"

My parents praised my performance as they gathered me in their arms. Dorothy clapped her little hands together as hard as she could. It was a blissful moment I would never forget.

At the end of the season, Miss Russell gave another recital. This one was not an ordinary recital, at least not to me. It would be held on the Carmel Theater stage, a neighborhood movie house on Santa Monica Boulevard near the dance studio. I desperately wanted to be a part of it, but Miss Russell told me, "You're too young, dear, maybe next year." That disappointed me.

The day of the recital, all the students who were not performing, plus their families, friends, and most of the neighborhood, poured into the theater and filled every seat. The performances went well, and the audience cheered and applauded. Then the girls brought Miss Russell out on the stage to take a bow. I was so proud of my beautiful teacher. How nice if I could be up there too, I thought, with the stage lights shining up on me.

When the theater darkened and the movie started, I couldn't take my eyes off the handsome leading actor. He wore a turban and lived in a big tent in the desert. Large cushions covered the floor. He dashed off on his horse where he swept up a pretty lady and carried her into his tent. She looked scared, and I couldn't figure out why.

Later, as we walked out of the theater, I chattered to Mother, "I can't wait until I'm a grown-up lady and a handsome man like that carries me off to his tent in the desert, then sits me on those comfy cushions. I wouldn't be frightened like that lady. I might even dance for him."

Mother laughed and told me that all the ladies were in love with that actor, and she agreed he was indeed, handsome.

To this day, when I remember that recital, I recall that movie and that handsome actor, Rudolph Valentino, who stole my little-girl heart.

## Chapter Two

One of my favorite childhood memories is that whenever Christmas came, Hollywood Boulevard turned into a fairyland known as Santa Claus Lane. I was six and Dorothy three, the first time our parents took us to see the parade. I remember Dorothy sat on Daddy's shoulders as we stood at the curb and waited for the parade to begin. Real pine trees with twinkling lights lined the boulevard. Later, they replaced them with fabricated facsimiles—pretty, but we missed the real ones. The parade started at Vine Street and continued west to Highland Avenue. I remember real reindeer pulled Santa's sled. Later, they loaded the sled on a flatbed truck with mechanical reindeer in front—not half as exciting. Santa would sit in his sleigh with a famous celebrity beside him while a fan blew fake snow over them. From then on we went to the parade every year.

There was no fake snow the morning Mother popped into our room and said, "Get up, girls, and look out the window."

We ran to the big bay window in the living room and could hardly believe what we saw. Snow. Real snow covered our lawn and driveway—and on Hollywood Boulevard. Accustomed to seeing snow-capped mountains from our home, we'd been to Camp Baldy where we played in the snow, but we never expected to see snow covering our house. Newspaper articles and photos of snow scenes appeared for days. News of our freak snowfall was on the radio for weeks.

I always dreaded getting colds. I suppose because mine weren't the ordinary kind that most kids got with the sniffling and sneezing then it passed. My colds never seemed to end. The wheezing started in my chest, and it became difficult for me to breathe unless I took in big gulps of air. They took me to a doctor, and after all the tests, which I hated, he told my parents, "Your child has asthma."

I didn't know at the time what that was. I only knew I missed school and dance lessons, and was miserable trying to breathe. My diagnosis upset Mother. I learned later that when she was only five years old, her mother, who was twenty-six, had died of asthma.

One doctor suggested that dry desert air might do me good. The damp, foggy nights in Hollywood certainly didn't help my condition. He had several patients, he said, who had been cured in the dry Palm Springs air.

A few nights later when my wheezing was really bad, Daddy wrapped me in a blanket, carried me out to the car, and gently placed me in the back seat next to Dorothy. "We're going to Palm Springs, out in the desert," he explained. "We have to drive at night. It's too hot to make the trip during the day. Cars can get overheated and radiators boil over."

I remember before we left, Daddy put some kind of contraption filled with blocks of ice and a fan on the side of the car by a window. "This will blow cool air into the car while we're driving," he said. Very primitive air-conditioning.

On our way to the desert, Daddy told Mother, "Now we have to go through Pomona, Ontario, Riverside, Beaumont, and Banning. The road to Palm Springs is a narrow road that goes through Cabazon and Whitewater before we reach the village." Then his voice faded away as I drifted off to a much needed sleep.

By morning the shining sun and warm dry air helped me breathe! What a relief. We checked into a little bungalow at Coble Court on Indian Avenue. Mr. Coble, the owner, had a huge tortoise that inched slowly around the grounds. Sometimes he'd let Dorothy ride on its back. A delightfully slow ride.

"It's so obvious," Daddy said, "that there's an improvement in Babe's condition. I'll come back and get you all next weekend. Meanwhile, thank God, she can breathe." Dorothy and I spent the days walking and running on the dirt road called Palm Canyon. Palm Springs was a quiet little village, and no one stayed there after May because of the heat. The Indians remained as full-time residents. There was just one hotel then, called the Desert Inn. When we walked by, we'd peek through the gate at the orange and grapefruit trees. Mother missed reading the morning paper because there wasn't any. A small, wooden structure on Indian Avenue contained hot mineral baths. Mr. Coble suggested we might like to give them a try, which we did. Indian ladies helped us as we stepped down into the hot water. It felt good to us kids as it bubbled up around us, leaving a tingly sensation.

Since we didn't have a phone, Mother used the one in the main store when she called Daddy. The store doubled as a post office where we would mail cards to Daddy. From there, we'd often walk down the road to the library to pick up some books so Mother could read to us in the evenings. I loved Palm Springs and was so happy to be breathing normally again.

We made many trips to the desert during the next several years and stayed at Coble Court. Every time I got a cold and the wheezing began, we packed up and made the nighttime trip to Palm Springs. I always felt better the moment we arrived. And each time we had to leave, I hated to go back to the damp, foggy nights away from the dry, warm air.

On one of our trips, Mr. Coble told Daddy he could buy an acre of land for two hundred dollars. I heard Daddy say, "Now what would I do with an acre of sand in this barren desert?"

Back home one morning at breakfast Mother announced, "We're going to move to another house." Daddy had been told about a pocket of dry air nestled close to the hills one block north of Hollywood Boulevard. "It won't be as dry as the desert," she said, "but there's no dampness or fog there at night. You'll have to change schools, but it will be worth it for your health."

The next afternoon we were on our way to see our new home. "This is it," Daddy said, as he parked at the curb. "This is our new house."

It set high up from the street with a lawn that sloped down to the sidewalk. I ran up the steps to the front porch and smiled when I saw the view. Daddy pointed to Catalina Island sitting out there in the ocean. Then he turned and pointed out Grauman's Chinese Theater on Hollywood Boulevard.

I thought, how wonderful to be this close to the movies. I loved our new home, and I would live there for the next twelve years. I never had another asthma attack.

I walked the six blocks to Gardner Street School, as I did at Laurel. I made many friends the first day. A week later my teacher discovered I'd been taking piano lessons for two years. She asked me if I'd play for the students when they marched into the auditorium for assembly. I agreed and was glad I'd been practicing every day. Since I had been playing "Nola" quite well, I thought the kids would enjoy that song as they filed in. Afterwards, I figured I could have played chopsticks, and they wouldn't have known the difference.

At home, I loved hearing the piano being played next door. We made friends with Barbara, the little girl who lived there. She told us that her daddy wrote songs. Every day we would see the same man visit our neighbor and we could hear the two of them singing catchy tunes. We had no idea then that such hit songs as "Temptation," "Pagan Love Song," and "Singin' in the Rain," were being born.

Many years later our former neighbor would become the most important producer of star-studded musicals at MGM—and unbeknownst to him—I would be dancing in some of them. When he'd visit on the set I would never approach him. I knew he'd never remember the nine-year-old little kid who once lived next door, loving the music that he, Arthur Freed, and Nacio Herb Brown, were composing.

One day Mother and I stood on the front lawn when a sporty little roadster came around the corner and drove past us, evidently headed for Hollywood Boulevard. "Why, that looks like Tom Brown, the young movie star," Mother said. "He must live up in the hills and is probably on his way to the studios." That impressed me to think that movie stars would be driving up and down our street.

The following day I sat out there on the grass hoping to see him again. Sure enough, the little roadster rounded the curve. I stood up and waved frantically. He saw me, grinned, and waved back. From then on, I often waited out there and waved to him as he drove by. Sometimes he waved first. I thought he was about the best-looking man I'd ever seen. Imagine, a movie star waving to me.

I filled the busy days with piano lessons, dancing lessons, playing for the school assembly, and dancing in school shows. I also wrote poems about everything and everyone.

Then my parents told us how important it was to learn how to swim. Neither of them had ever learned, and they were sorry. So Dorothy and I were enrolled in the Carl Curtis Swimming School. Carl was not only a marvelous swimmer, but a big, strong, handsome man. I didn't like it, though, when he said it was necessary to put my face underwater as we practiced the American Crawl. But

I would have done anything to become a good swimmer and make Carl proud of me. Later he told my mother, "She's learning very quickly for a nine-year-old."

Then came the day when Carl told me to dive off the side of the pool. He showed me the correct position, then said, "Go!" I took a deep breath and dove in. When I came up, he smiled. "You're ready for the low board now," he said. I practiced my dives, and Carl seemed pleased with my progress, which made me happy.

I was ten when our family spent a few days at a place called Glenn Ranch, somewhere in the California Mountains. Small cabins were nestled under the trees, with a brook running through the property. Other families had children too, so we had friends to play with. A wonderful place to vacation. I practiced my swimming and diving off the side of their pool. The only problem, as far as I was concerned, was they had no low board, only a high one. But, I thought, since I know how to dive, it will be the same, only higher. I wanted to try it.

Several people swam in the pool—others sat casually around the side. I had a captive audience. Cautiously I climbed up the ladder, one rung at a time. I waved to Dorothy below while mustering up the courage to step on the high board. But Dorothy didn't wave. She motioned for me to come down. I waved to her again and saw her run—to find Mother. I thought, if I'm going to make this dive, I'd better do it before they get back. I stepped on the board and walked to the edge. My heart pumped hard as I looked down at the water. It appeared much farther away than I expected. I wondered if I could hold my breath long enough to dive and reach the surface again. I backed up from the edge and looked down again. Mother and Dorothy frantically waved for me to come down. Everyone around the pool looked up. What to do? My audience awaited, and I'd have been embarrassed to leave after standing up there for so long. I got scared just thinking about it, but I remembered how Carl taught me to dive off the low board. Of course, the water wasn't nearly so far away then. I wondered what Carl would have said to me if he'd been there. I stepped to the edge of the board. I didn't dare look at Mother, or Dorothy, or all the others. I had to do it. I got into my diving position, gave one more scary glance at the water below, and then took in as much air as my lungs would hold. I pictured Carl there, saying, "Go!" I dove in—feeling the rush of cold water as I slid under. My toes touched bottom. A moment later I crashed to the surface, gasping for air. Everyone clapped, and the kids cheered. I could only think, I did it! I did it! But deep inside I knew I could.

# Chapter Three

It was a rainy Saturday, a good day to sit by the fire, drink cocoa, and read from my book, *The Little Colonel*, handsomely bound in pink silk. I was always glad to receive a book in that series for Christmas and on my birthdays. I enjoyed them more than the *Nancy Drew* books which were very popular with my school friends.

If it hadn't been raining, I might have been across the street visiting my girlfriend. We often climbed up the big avocado tree in her backyard, and I would read to her while nibbling on a delicious avocado. I felt so close to that tree, almost as if it was my second home. Maybe that's why I'm so fond of avocados.

But there were no avocados that day, nothing but rain, and my book. Dorothy sat with me when Mother entered the room and announced, "How would you girls like to see the Russian ballet at the Philharmonic Auditorium? There's a matinee next Saturday." It sounded wonderful, and I could hardly wait.

When Saturday arrived, we took the streetcar on Hollywood Boulevard to downtown Los Angeles. Dorothy and I felt very grown up in our favorite dresses and white gloves. Little ladies, we were told, always wore white gloves when going to the theater. Before the performance, we ate lunch in a little tea room where a lady entertained us with organ music. After dessert we walked to the Philharmonic. The ballerinas, considered the best in the world, danced "Swan Lake" that day. One of the dancers, Irena Baronova, was so exquisite she mesmerized me. We guessed her to be about eighteen or nineteen years old. I was so taken by the ballet costumes, the lighting that bathed the stage in moonlight, and the graceful dancers, I decided then that I wanted to dance in a ballet company.

Yes, I always knew I wanted to be a dancer. And I was sure what my little sister wanted to be—an actress. Dorothy was always so quiet and shy that if I didn't take her by the hand and drag her around with me, she wouldn't have moved. I loved her very much, but she was "Little Miss Sobersides," the serious one.

When we put on shows for the neighborhood kids, Dorothy played in the sad or dramatic scene. They were often so touching that some of the kids would wipe tears away. I thought she'd become a great dramatic actress. She seldom laughed out loud, but a little smile would trickle across her face when something amused her. She was easy to get along with and quite happy to tag along with me.

Dorothy and I were playing in our bedroom one day with our dolls when Mother called out to us, "Girls!" We joined her in the living room where she sat staring out the window. As we entered, she said, "Sit down here beside me and listen very carefully to what I have to tell you. Daddy just phoned from the Stock Exchange, where he works. The stock market has crashed."

I tried to imagine what that would mean to us when she continued. "It means that many men will lose their jobs, and people who had money won't have it anymore. You'll hear a lot of talk now about the crash, but I don't want you girls to worry. We will always have food, although most of our meals will be soup and sandwiches. No more meat or desserts. We'll always have a place to live, and hopefully, we can remain here. We don't know how long Daddy will have his job. Piano, dancing, and swimming lessons will have to stop for now. We will have to cut down on everything."

"Don't worry," Dorothy said, looking very concerned, "I'll get a job."

"Honey, it won't be necessary for a seven-year-old to get a job, but it's sweet of you to offer." Mother smiled, and so did I at Dorothy's innocent little face when she offered to help.

We all knew there would be some rough days ahead—for us, and everyone. The newspapers and radio stations carried stories about people and the crash of 1929. Those who could afford to go to a movie theater and catch the newsreel would see long lines of the unemployed, standing outside the soup kitchens, and others trying to sell apples on street corners. If you didn't have money for the movies, a friend would go and report back about what they had seen. Desperate men jumped from high buildings because they lost all their money. Others shot and killed themselves. It was a terrible time.

Dorothy and I were playing in the backyard one day when a tired-looking man with several days' growth of whiskers trudged up our steep driveway to the back door. He knocked, and Mother came to the door. We couldn't hear what he said, but Mother went back into the house while the man sat on the step.

Minutes later, Mother came out of the house and handed the man a tray with a bowl of soup and a sandwich. After he had finished eating, he set the tray down and left. He didn't seem to notice us girls at all. It happened quite often, men coming to our house for food. But Mother always had a large pot of soup simmering on the stove. She handed out many bowls of her soup and a sandwich to those in need.

One day Daddy noticed a chalk-mark in the shape of an arrow on the sidewalk at the foot of our driveway. We wondered what that meant. Later, a neighbor told us it was to notify others they could get food at our home.

In 1930, when I was eleven, I graduated from Gardner Street Grammar School. When our teacher said we'd need a song for our graduating class, I put some lyrics to "Lazy Bones," which we all sang:

Gardner school, we are all for you
Every student from the old to new
These words are ringing through the hall
You're the school that beats them all

Dorothy graduated three years later. "Guess what, Sis," she said, "we're singing your song and our teacher let me stand on a chair and lead the class because she knew I was your sister."

Entering Bancroft Junior High was an exciting time for me—new classes, new rules, new friends, and more than one teacher. It was too far to walk, so my mother and a neighbor took turns driving her daughter and me to school every morning. Bancroft had a reputation for having students with a clean-cut image. Girls weren't allowed to wear makeup as they did at Le Conte Junior High. We all looked very wholesome in our dresses, skirts and blouses, white socks and saddle shoes.

And we discovered boys. "Who is that swell-looking boy on campus? What's his name?"

"I found out his name," said one of the girls. "And he's so handsome, I'll bet some day he'll be a movie star."

"Well, what's his name?" we all asked.

"It's Gower Champion."

At the time, we had no idea that he'd be half the dance team of Marge and Gower Champion. He would go on to become a famous choreographer and director of Broadway hits like *Bye Bye Birdie* and *Hello, Dolly!*

When the music teacher learned that I played the piano, she

asked me one day, "Would you be willing to accompany the Glee Club, instead of singing? We don't have an accompanist right now and it would be wonderful if you would do this for us. We're going to sing for the PTA next month in the auditorium. The curtain will open with the piano on stage. You will walk on and sit at the piano while the singers file in and take their positions. Then you'll accompany them while they sing three songs. When we finish, you will get up, take a bow, then follow the singers off stage." I told her I would be happy to play for them.

I was thrilled, of course, and told Mother all about it when I got home that day. She was so happy for me. I certainly didn't want to make any mistakes, so I practiced at home, an hour every day on those three songs. I was overjoyed that I had taken piano lessons and heeded the advice of my teacher, Mrs. Wallis, to practice.

During study period one day, a boy in my class walked by and dropped a note on my desk. When I opened it later, he had written in pencil: "If you know how to screw, meet me after school."

Being rather naive, I didn't know what he had in mind. I took the note home and showed it to Mother. The way her eyes narrowed as she shook her head told me something was not right. "Where did you get this?" she demanded. When I told her, she looked very angry, and later I overheard her discussing it with Daddy. I could only catch part of their conversation, but I heard Mother say, "It's disgraceful to think that a child of that age is writing notes like that." Daddy agreed.

The next day, after Mother drove us to school, she had a talk with the principal. That boy never wrote me a note like that again.

For my thirteenth birthday, I invited thirteen of my girlfriends to a luncheon at our home. Mother told me, "Your friends will bring you gifts, and it would be nice for them to receive little gifts from you." We bought thirteen bracelets studded with little beads and placed them as favors for each guest.

Mother baked two large chocolate cakes: one for my party and one for our annual trip to the orphanage. The orphanage consisted of individual bungalows; each housed eight girls, according to age. Since I was thirteen, we would take the cake to the bungalow that held the thirteen-year-olds. Two months before, when Dorothy was ten, we took a cake to those who were ten-year-olds. We were always taught, "It's important to share with others."

Mother often took us to the movie matinees at Grauman's Egyptian Theater. This had been the first theater Sid Grauman built on Hollywood Boulevard. Little shops lined the courtyard, and we loved to look in them before entering the theater. I always admired the theater interior with all the ornate columns and the huge sphinxes beside the stage, similar to the ones in my geography school book. After the show we'd be treated to an ice cream soda at the Pig'n Whistle next door.

On the nights when they held premieres, we could see the searchlights from our home. We imagined how glamorous it must be for the movie fans awaiting the arrival of the stars in their limousines. We could only read about it in the papers the next day. Daddy had taken Mother to see the first movie that opened there—*Robin Hood*, starring Douglas Fairbanks, Sr.

When *Hell's Angels*, starring Jean Harlow, premiered at Grauman's Chinese Theater, our parents didn't permit us to see it. It was a war movie. But the following day, they allowed us to walk to the theater and see the World War I fighter planes suspended above the forecourt. I saw the open cockpits and imagined fighter pilots sitting in there, shooting at the enemy. It seemed terrifying to me, and yet, I was excited at the thought.

Everyone gossiped about Clara Bow, the actress they called the "It" girl—a sexy, free-spirited vamp who supposedly had "It," what every man desired in a woman, and every woman enviously wished she had.

One day I told Mother, "Clara Bow is playing in her new movie, *Call Her Savage*, at the Egyptian, and I want to see it."

"Babe," she said, "that movie is not suitable for a girl your age. There are other movies you can see."

But I was determined to see this "It" girl who everyone was raving about. Since study period was my last class, I decided to leave school one afternoon, take the streetcar to Hollywood Boulevard, then walk to the movie. I'd still get out in time to arrive home, and no one would know where I'd been. Luckily, I had sixty cents for the streetcar and the movie. I was excited that day, as I slipped into the darkened theater—the movie had already begun. I didn't care because there she was, the "It" girl, Clara Bow. I wasn't quite sure what it was about, but just seeing her there on the screen was a stolen thrill. Fortunately, Mother and Daddy never found out.

I was crazy about actor Buddy Rogers and when I watched his movies, I wished I could have been his leading lady instead of Nancy Carroll. I didn't know then that over sixty years later, I would meet him in Palm Springs and receive an autographed picture that hangs on my wall to this day, satisfying that thirteen-year-old in me.

There were always birthday parties being held, either at school, or a friend's home. Usually they were held on a Friday or Saturday evening to avoid interfering with our school work and parents of the host or hostess always attended. The party started about seven and ended by ten. Most parents took their daughters to these parties, then picked them up afterwards.

At one of these parties, instead of the usual games of "pin the tail on the donkey" or "musical chairs," someone suggested we play "spin the bottle." We were all full of food, punch, and birthday cake, and thought it would be a wonderful game to play to finish off the evening.

Still rather naive as a budding teenager, I said, "I don't know what to do. How do you play this game?"

"You mean you've never played this before?" asked one of the girls. "Well," she explained, "we all sit on the floor in a circle, then a boy spins the bottle. When it stops spinning, whoever the bottle is pointing to, is the girl he gets to kiss. Then the next boy takes his turn. If it should stop and point to another boy, he can spin again. You'll see."

It sounded like fun to me. Then the game started, and a boy spun the bottle. I watched it spin and slowly come to a stop facing me. He gave me a kiss. I immediately liked this game. We continued playing, and I got lots of kisses.

Then someone suggested we play "post office." Everyone agreed, but this was also new to me. I had a lot to learn. I wondered how I ever got to be this old and not know how to play these fun games. Then the same girl explained. "The boy playing postman steps into the next room. Then he calls out, 'I have a Special Delivery letter for'—and names a girl he wants to kiss. She then steps into the room with him to get her 'letter.' Then another boy is the postman. See?"

I watched as, one by one, the girls got a call from the postman. Then I heard a boy call my name. I thought I knew what to expect after having played spin the bottle, so I stepped into the next room. This boy, Charlie, put his arms around me and pulled me tight to his body. He slowly bent me backwards in his arms, then I felt his lips on mine for a very long time. When it was over, I was overwhelmed. My heart was pounding, and I thought, wow, Charlie, that was just like in the movies. Yes, I'll always remember Charlie, and that kiss. We joined the others and the next postman was taking his turn when the host's mother entered and said to me. "Your father has arrived." I looked at my watch, ten o'clock, exactly. Darn. Why did he always have to be so punctual?

Walking along Hollywood Boulevard on Saturday mornings was a treat for me. I liked to visit Grauman's Chinese Theater and step into the footprints of the stars. They were all larger than my size 4B. I would rub my hand over the cement imprints and wish they were mine. Down the street was the Warner Brothers Theater. Across the street was Grauman's Egyptian.

I remember one day as I walked by, the movie *42nd Street* was playing. In the outer lobby were full-size cutouts of the gorgeous showgirls appearing in the film. I stood next to one. I was barely five-feet, and they were all taller than me, even when I stood on my tiptoes.

Woolworth's Five-and-Ten-Cent Store, where I bought my school supplies, was across the street. Nearby, the Dyas Department Store at Hollywood and Vine, later known as the Broadway Hollywood, was the place we bought all of our clothes.

The studios shot movie scenes all over Hollywood. A holiday or weekend was always a good day for a bank scene. They went on location everywhere, even in private homes. One day they used one of my friend's home. How fascinating to watch them set up all the lights and cameras. Little did I realize then that I'd be seeing a lot of that in the future.

In those days, many people came to Hollywood, hoping they might be used in some street scene and recognized as a future star. The Chamber of Commerce, however, published ads in the local papers warning people of the futility of trying to break into the movies. The ads mentioned that only one out of a thousand would reach the top. I often thought about that—only one in a thousand—not very good odds.

One beautiful day on my Saturday walk, I went to the Pantages Theater, near Vine Street. It had the largest stage of all the theaters and, at that time, hosted the Academy Awards ceremony.

Daddy sometimes treated me to lunch at the nearby Brown Derby restaurant on Vine Street. It was a very popular place, and most celebrities or movie stars ate lunch there and conducted a little business on the side. In fact, it was the first restaurant to have individual phone service. If you were a film star and a call came in for you, a waiter would bring a phone and plug it in at your table.

At times, actors would be there in makeup, often being interviewed while having lunch before rushing back to work. Fans would stand outside to see the stars as they entered and departed.

One day when Daddy and I left after lunch, we overheard a lady saying, "Oh, they're nobody."

That's Hollywood.

As I headed home, I often stopped at C.C. Browns, next to Grauman's Chinese Theater. They made the best hot fudge sundae in the whole--or at least in my world. They didn't pour the hot fudge over the ice cream as was usually done, but served it in a small pitcher so you could pour it yourself. So deliciously thick, it streamed down like honey. No wonder they were so famous.

Afterwards, I passed the Hollywood Hotel at the corner of Highland and Hollywood Boulevard. Beautiful palm trees shaded the entrance as guests mingled on the terrace.

Hollywood had its characters, and one of them certainly had to be "Peter the Hermit," with his flowing white hair, white shirt, white trousers, and sandals. We knew he lived alone in the Hollywood Hills. We never saw him with anyone, but he appeared to be very friendly. Everyone in town knew him and waved as he walked by. I always thought there was something magical about him.

It was March 10, 1933, and I looked forward to a party that evening. Mother suggested I lie down and rest that afternoon, so I'd be fresh for the party. I could hardly relax, thinking about my new dress and a certain boy who'd also been invited. In bed, I tossed and turned I was so excited.

At one point, I turned over so hard the bed shook, and kept shaking.

Mother rushed to my door and shouted, "It's an earthquake! Hurry and get up—stand in the doorway!" The floor moved under me as I headed for the door. Everything tumbled off the bureau and pictures fell off the walls. I stood in the doorway and held onto the framework, while my body shook along with the house. I was terrified and still shook after everything else had stopped. The radio announcer said it was a 6.3 on the Richter scale—a major quake. It caused a lot of damage and a few deaths. Needless to say, there was no party that night, and our earthquake was the topic of conversation for a long time thereafter.

# Chapter Four

Mother enrolled me in a dance class with Muriel Stuart, a protégée of the world-famous ballet dancer Anna Pavlova, as my teacher. I became one of her protégées. For the demanding training, arm and leg positions had to be exactly correct, toes pointed just so. It wasn't easy, but I loved it because I was determined to be a ballerina.

We held our first public performance in the Redlands Bowl, two and a half hours east of Hollywood. We left in the morning and rehearsed most of the day up until the evening performance. Our rehearsals went well, and we performed admirably. We arrived home tired, but assured we were a success our first time out.

One day, in the middle of our class, we were presented to a gentleman associated with the famous European director, Max Reinhardt. He chose four of us to dance in the production of Shakespeare's *A Midsummer Night's Dream*, to be played in the Hollywood Bowl. They held rehearsals in a large studio on Hollywood Boulevard. The studio head, Theodore Kosloff, danced in Pavlova's Company. He had large classes, and many of his students had gone on to ballet companies. Mr. Kosloff, a tough but respected taskmaster, carried a cane during classes and thumped it on the floor in time to the music.

One of the students told me, "When we do the barre work, if

your legwork isn't correct, he will hit you with the cane—not hard, but hard enough to let you know that you'd better correct your mistake and get it right." I thought, no wonder Russia turns out the best ballet dancers, if their methods are so strict.

This wasn't just a recital. This Shakespearian play in the Hollywood Bowl included well-known actors and featured Mickey Rooney playing the part of Puck, and we fairies would dance all around him. We rehearsed several hours a day practicing our fairy dance. In the dressing room after rehearsals, we talked excitedly about the wonderful opportunity to dance in a Max Reinhardt production.

I remember pleading with Mother, "Please take me to Max Factor for makeup and false eyelashes."

"Babe," she said, "you'll be dancing so far away from the audience no one will be able to see your eyes, let alone your eyelashes."

"But this is so important to me," I said. "It's my first appearance in the Hollywood Bowl. How can I perform without false eyelashes?"

I didn't care if the audience couldn't see my eyelashes, I'd know I was wearing them, and that was very important to me.

Mother soon realized how much those lashes meant to me, so several days later, off we went to the Max Factor salon on Highland Avenue.

We continued rehearsing at the Kosloff studio until a few days before the opening because the set designers hadn't completed the forest scene. The first day we rehearsed in the Bowl, I didn't recognize it.

In the past, Dorothy and I had been to the Hollywood Bowl many evenings to hear the symphonies. Our parents wanted us to become familiar with the classical music of famous composers. We'd sit on the benches in the amphitheater and look down at the orchestra on the stage—the huge shell looming up behind them.

But that first day of rehearsal, where was the Bowl? It was nowhere in sight. In its place was a big grass-covered hill with bushes and trees. The designers had built a forest that blended in with the natural hills in the background. We fairies were to dance around Puck on the top of the hill. I didn't mind our lengthy and tiring rehearsals. Instead of being in the audience as I'd been in the past, I was now on stage, appearing in the Hollywood Bowl—my first professional appearance.

The September weather was cool and balmy. The symphony orchestra played Felix Mendelssohn's "Midsummer Night's Dream," that to this day is my favorite. Whenever I hear it, I can visualize the whole production as I saw it from the hilltop. Searchlights pierced the sky like theater opening nights. Many movie stars attended the performance. What a twist I thought—now I was on stage, and they were watching *me*. As the show started, I crouched behind the bushes with the other fairies and Puck as we waited for our cue to dance. Mickey Rooney was a perfect Puck; small, full of energy, and his Puckish laugh fit so well with his character. No one else could have played that role better than he did. While we waited in the dark for the lights to shine on us, Mickey told jokes that caused us fairies to giggle. During rehearsals, he would pat our bottoms when we didn't expect it. But we forgave him because he was so cute and so much fun. A bright light suddenly lit up the top of the hill and like magic, we little fairies danced on the hilltop. The play finished to thunderous applause with Puck's famous closing lines:

And so goodnight to you all
Give me your hands if we be friends
And Robin shall restore amends.

The show received excellent reviews, and we played another few weeks with sold-out performances. When Warner Brothers made it into a movie, the young, unknown actress with the big brown eyes who played the role of Hermia would also play that part in the movie version. A few months later I wasn't surprised to hear that Olivia de Havilland was signed to a seven-year contract with Warner Brothers.

I continued classes with Mr. Kosloff since Miss Stuart no longer taught. Mr. Kosloff, always the perfectionist, watched every move his students made like a hawk. For some, it paid off. One girl in our class later became part of the dance team, The DeMarcos.

Sometimes Mr. Kosloff scared me, and other times I wanted to hug him. My barre work improved, and so did my technique. I eventually considered myself a Kosloff dancer. And as one of his dancers, I appeared in *The Nights of Pompeii*, a large spectacle held in the Los Angeles Coliseum.

A diminutive fiery lady with dark flashing eyes and black hair named Carmelita Marrachi, taught a Spanish and Gypsy dancing class at the studio. With my parents' permission, I enrolled with several other girls from Kosloff's class for the opportunity to learn another type of dance.

Carmelita was a strict teacher and her dancing was stylish and inspiring. It wasn't easy to train my fingers to rapidly click the castanets, but the stamping of the feet and the fast clicking of the heels on the floor came easy to me. I found the music and the wild dramatic dance to be very exciting—and I felt fortunate to have learned from such a brilliant dancer as Carmelita.

After graduating from Bancroft Junior High, I attended Hollywood High School. Now aged fifteen, I met kids from two different junior highs and couldn't believe the makeup some of those girls wore. I felt plain and pale beside them and their bright red lipstick.

After checking in, they assigned us rooms, subjects, and teachers. Girls from the senior class showed us freshman girls around campus. "If you have any problems," one of them said, "just let us know. We're your big sisters and here to help you."

When I arrived home after that first day my mother asked, "How did it go today, Babe?"

"Fine," I said. "But I have to buy some bright red lipstick—high school girls wear makeup."

"Tangee is a good lipstick and has a nice natural-looking color," she said.

"But I don't want a natural color, Mother—all the girls are wearing bright red."

That evening, Daddy drove me to the drugstore. I bought a Tangee lipstick for school the next day. But the next morning when I put it on, I was disappointed. "What kind of lipstick is this?" I asked my mother. "No matter how thick I put it on, it's still pale looking. It doesn't look like I'm wearing any at all."

She told me it looked healthy instead of cheap. I still didn't like it.

When I entered the girls' restroom, in front of all the mirrors were the girls from Bancroft Junior High applying their bright red lipstick.

One girl told me, "This morning I stopped at the drugstore on the way to school and bought mine. My mom doesn't know. She thinks I'm wearing the Tangee she bought for me yesterday." Then she offered me hers to try. "Here," she said. "Try mine until you get your own."

I put some on my fingertip, dabbed it on my lips, and now felt like a high school girl. The girls told me they took it off before they got home.

I felt lucky to join Mr. Kachel's drama class. His productions were considered very professional—and agents and talent scouts often sat in the audience. Miss Heap, the dance teacher, had classes a student could join rather than taking gym. I entered her class also.

During lunch hour, I ate quickly so I could spend the rest of the time hanging out the window of an empty upstairs classroom. Looking down on the quad, I could see the guys in their senior sweaters surrounding the usual clique of beautiful girls. They would be flirting and laughing. It appeared that one would have to be beautiful to join that group.

One of the girls, Judy Turner, was a very pretty brunette. I heard later that she ditched one of her classes to get a Coke at the Top Hat Café (not Schwabs' drugstore) across from the school. While there, the editor of *The Hollywood Reporter* spotted her and asked how she'd like to be in the movies. She remained a brunette for her first two parts. Then MGM signed her, made her a blonde, changed her name to Lana, and turned her into a glittering star.

Other girls in school and in my classes also became famous, such as Alexis Smith and Nanette Fabares (Fabray). One of my class-mates, Joe Wapner, later became known as "Judge Wapner," of *The People's Court* TV show.

Mr. Kachel scheduled a production, and I wanted the part of the "Red Menace." The role called for an actress to wear a tight red gown, slit up the side to the knee. She also carried a long, cigarette holder. It wasn't the lead, but I was drooling to play the part. In the past I'd always been cast as the "sweet little ingénue."

"Mr. Kachel," I pleaded, "please let me play that part."

He smiled and I caught a twinkle in his eye. "Think you can do it?"

"Oh yes, I want that part so much," I pleaded.

"I think you can do it too," he said. "The part's yours."

I hugged him and couldn't think of anything else the rest of the day. I kept saying to myself, "I'm going to be the Red Menace—a real vamp, like the 'It' girl."

As usual, that show succeeded, and I felt so sexy, slithering on stage, as I held that cigarette holder between my fingers. The next morning one of my friends told me, "I didn't know you when you came on stage. We couldn't believe that little you could look so sexy."

That remark made it all worthwhile.

I not only acted in plays, I also appeared in the school musicals. *The Red Mill*, a popular one, became a big hit with the audience. In another show, Margery Belcher and a girl named Jane Mueller and I danced together dressed as artists, carrying brushes and palettes. The three of us danced the same steps in our toe shoes, then one-by-one, we would come forward for a quick solo.

Jane's solo was doing leaps around the stage. She could leap higher than most dancers I had seen. I performed pirouettes. When it was Marge's turn, she went up on her toes, did a backbend, and traveled in tiny steps, backward across the stage. I wondered how she could do that—I know I couldn't—she was amazing. And obviously that boy from Bancroft, Gower Champion, thought so too. Later, they were married and became a famous dance team.

As my sixteenth birthday approached, I invited eight boys and seven girls to my "Sweet Sixteen" party. The invitations, sent out weeks in advance, requested, "No gifts."

After school one day, Mother took me shopping for my birthday gown. As soon as I stepped out of the store elevator, a beautiful "knockout" gown caught my eye. It was a bright, lipstick-red, silk crepe, with red ostrich feathers on the shoulders. This was for me, I thought. I showed it to my mother as she was looking at an assortment of gowns on the rack.

"Mother," I said. "This is the one I want for my birthday party. Isn't it beautiful?"

She looked at the gown, and then looked at me. "Babe," she said, "that gown is just not your type. It would look ridiculous on you." She pointed to another. "Now here's one that's perfect." She held up soft, pale-blue chiffon, with a flowing skirt, a blue-satin collar at the neck and tiny rhinestone buttons that ran down the front. At the waist, the buttons met a narrow blue-satin belt with a rhinestone buckle.

"I don't want that one," I protested. "I won't feel sixteen. I love this red one and look at all the fluffy, red ostrich feathers."

A saleslady approached and asked if she could help. I told her I liked the red gown for my birthday, but my mother liked the blue. I asked her what she thought.

"Well," she said, "I'll have to agree with your mother that the blue one is more suitable if you're going to be fourteen."

"But I'll be sixteen," I snapped back.

"Oh, I'm sorry, dear. I guessed you to be about fourteen. You're very young looking. I still think the blue is preferable."

I couldn't help but think, what's the matter with this woman? She ought to be fired. But I took both dresses to the dressing room to try them on. The blue one fit, but reminded me of the song, "Sweet Little Alice Blue Gown." I wasn't at all excited about it and couldn't wait to try on the red one.

I slipped into it, looked in the mirror, and said, "Boy, look at me, I'm the Red Menace all over again. All I need is my cigarette holder." I wanted it so bad.

When Mother saw it on me, she said, "Honey, that gown is not right for you. You heard what the saleslady said."

Well, you can guess which one we took home.

How disappointed I was that I would not be as dazzling and sexy as I wanted to be for this special night!

On the morning of April 6, 1935, I woke up, and was sixteen years old. In preparation for my party that night, Daddy rolled up the carpets so we could dance on the bare wood floor. We set up four card tables with chairs for the guests and covered them with tablecloths and decorations. I put sixteen place cards strategically around the tables, knowing which boys liked to sit with which girls.

While Daddy blew up balloons, I chose records for the dancing. The living room had the feel of a nightclub. Mother had been preparing dishes and had baked three of her fabulous chocolate cakes. Dorothy helped decorate them. Two cakes were for my party, and the other we would take to the orphanage the next day. I knew it'd be a wonderful evening, especially since my boyfriend from USC would be there to make it perfect.

The party started at seven and was to continue until eleven. My parents elected to stay in the kitchen to afford us some privacy. At five o'clock, I showered and put on that stupid blue dress, and waited for my guests. Dorothy wound up the handle on the Victrola and put on a stack of records I had chosen.

At seven, the guests began to arrive. The girls looked beautiful in their gowns, and the boys looked especially handsome in their suits. They wished me a happy birthday and complimented me on my gown. I thought, sure, they're just being nice.

When my favorite boyfriend arrived, he looked so handsome. Then he said to me, "You look beautiful tonight, and I love that gown. Blue is my favorite color."

Well, I thought, maybe this gown isn't so bad after all!

My guests dined and danced, and I felt quite beautiful and happy knowing that blue was his favorite color. Then the doorbell rang, and my last guest arrived. I opened the door, and there she stood in that red gown with the fluffy red ostrich feathers. Oh no, I couldn't believe it! That gown should have been mine. But I greeted her warmly and tried to smile as the red feathers waved to me on her way to the living room. I thought, of all the gowns she could have bought, why did she have to choose that one? The one I wanted so much.

Then my boyfriend asked me to dance, and while we were on the floor, I called his attention to the red gown and asked if he liked it.

"You mean the one with the goofy red feathers?" he asked. Then his voice lowered. "I don't think it's hers. She must have borrowed it from her mother."

"Are you serious?" I said. "You mean you don't like it?"

"Naw," he told me, "I like yours. It looks like you."

"Looks like me? And the red one with the goofy feathers? You think she borrowed it from her mother?" I said, stunned.

When the party ended, they all thanked me for a wonderful evening. My boyfriend, the last to leave, kissed me goodnight and whispered, "You look beautiful in that gown. I love you."

It was a great evening for me, and what he said as he left, made it perfect . . . a night to remember.

# Chapter Five

One evening, our parents' favorite friends, Arthur and Mae Miller, came for their weekly visit. Artie, considered one of Hollywood's best cameramen, always entertained us. His career began in 1914 when he filmed the famous serial, *The Perils of Pauline*. Later, he would receive Academy Awards for *How Green Was My Valley*, *The Song of Bernadette*, and *Anna and the King of Siam*. His visits always included rather flamboyant descriptions of events on the set of his present movie. Dorothy and I were crazy about him and the way he'd mimic the characters he filmed. It was like being there on the set with them. So often, he would have us doubled up with laughter, playing all the different roles. According to Artie, Dorothy and I were always his best audience. We thought he should have been an actor.

On this particular evening, after chatting for about an hour, we sat anxiously waiting for Artie to entertain us. He told us about *Pigskin Parade*, an almost completed movie, and this kid that concerned him. "She only has a few more days of shooting," he said. "She's very talented and has a great personality. We've become close enough on the set so she feels comfortable talking with me. It was obvious to me that she was very lonely."

We'd never heard Artie speak of any actor before with such concerns. He continued, "Well, this kid can't wait for her part in the picture to be over so she can attend public school. She's very excited that she'll be attending Bancroft Junior High, even if it's only for a short time before her next film." Artie turned to me. "Babe, she can't wait to get to Hollywood High like you."

Then Artie spoke to my sister. "Dorothy, since you go to Bancroft, I'd like to tell this girl that a friend of mine will be looking her up. You're both the same age, so you will probably be in the same grade. Her name is Judy Garland."

"Artie," Mother said, "the girls are always free to invite their school friends for dinner or sleepovers. And if Judy would like that, she's certainly welcome."

"That would be wonderful," he said.

A week later Dorothy told us, "I inquired about Judy on the campus today so I'd know which girl she was. I found her at recess where she was standing with several other girls. I went over to her, and when I told her I was Artie Miller's friend, she was real happy to see me. She loves Artie as much as we do."

The next time Artie and Mae visited us, they asked how Judy was getting along at school.

"She's having a great time," said Dorothy. "We all love her sense of humor, and when she laughs, it's so contagious we find ourselves laughing with her. But we were worried when she was called into the office of the girls' vice-principal."

"What on earth for?" I asked.

"The lipstick thing. Remember, Sis, I told you. She's been coming to school wearing lipstick, and she knows the rules about no makeup. Her teachers have been warning her about it all week, but she's ignored them.

"We all wondered how long she would get away with it. Three of us waited for her outside in the hall. We hated to see her in trouble.

When the door opened and she came out, we could see that her lipstick had been wiped off. Then before we even had a chance to ask what happened in there, she opened her purse, took out her lipstick, and put it on again."

Artie looked very concerned. "I wondered how she'd get along in public school. She thought it would give her the freedom to be like the other kids, but how could she expect to be like them when she's been in show business since she was a little tyke. She's old beyond her years. She probably thought it was stupid to make such a fuss about lipstick when she's been wearing it since she was about two or three." Artie shook his head as he thought about Judy's difficulty adjusting.

Two weeks later, when Daddy picked up Dorothy after school, Judy was with her to spend the evening and sleep-over. When they arrived, I was on my way out to a ballet lesson.

Later, when I returned home, I was in a hurry to get ready for a dinner and dancing date that night. Unfortunately, I didn't have much opportunity to spend any time with Dorothy and her friend. The following evening I asked Dorothy if she and Judy had a good time.

"Yes, it was real nice. She loved playing with the dogs. She hugged and petted them and said how much she loved animals. Then Mother said she would bake a lemon pie for dinner, and Judy helped me pick some lemons off our tree. After dinner, Daddy made a fire in the fireplace. We toasted marshmallows and drank hot cocoa, like we often do, but it was new to Judy."

"You know what she told me, Sis?" Dorothy smiled as she continued. "Dorothy, you're so lucky because you have a real family."

The question of college came up one day. "No, Mother and Daddy, I don't want to go to college," I told them. "What's the point of being a dancer if I'm not going to dance? I'm almost eighteen, and going to that new college, UCLA, would be a waste of my time. Besides, if I had to, I'd rather go to good old USC."

"All right," Daddy said. "If you feel that strongly about it. But consider this: you graduate in January—it will be college for you in the fall term unless you get a dance job before that—is that fair enough?"

"Yes, that's fair." I gave them each a hug.

On graduation day, all I could think of was, I've got to get a job dancing. I've just got to. After the ceremonies, everyone said their goodbyes. They hugged and cried and wished each other "Good luck." A very pretty girl with blonde curls waved goodbye to me—I didn't know her well—she had only been in one of my classes. I asked her if she planned to go to college.

"No," she answered. "I'm going to continue working in the movie studios."

"What do you do?" I asked.

"Dance."

"Dance? I didn't know you could dance," I said. "Why didn't you ever dance in our school shows?"

"Too busy dancing in pictures," she said. "I had to miss some school, but I've been tutored."

"How wonderful! That's what I want to do—dance in the movies like you. What do I do?"

"Go to dance auditions. If you like, I'll let you know when they'll be having another one. Give me your phone number."

I was so excited I couldn't remember my own number. I told her, "You give me yours, and I'll call you when I get home, okay?"

I couldn't believe all this. I just knew I was going to dance in the movies. What a lucky break. I'll go on an audition, then have a dance job. I won't have to go to college. I couldn't wait to tell my parents.

A few days later the phone rang, and she told me, "There's going to be a dance audition some time next week at MGM. I'll let you know the date and time. It's a big musical starring Eleanor Powell and Nelson Eddy called *Rosalie*. I'll be there too," she added.

"What do I wear? How should I look?" I asked.

"Bring your ballet slippers and a practice outfit."

I couldn't sleep that night. I pictured myself dancing in the movies. No college. It was absolutely wonderful. I could hardly wait for the week to go by, wondering when my friend would call.

Then one day when I returned from my ballet lesson, my mother said, "Your friend called. It was about that audition."

I called her back, then ran to tell my mother, "It's tomorrow. I know I won't be able to sleep tonight. I'm going to dance in the movies!"

Mother drove me to MGM. It seemed like such a long drive, over an hour to Culver City from our house. When we finally arrived, Mother dropped me off at the gate, then waited to drive me back home.

Hundreds of girls jammed the large soundstage. I thought, so this is an audition? I couldn't even find my school friend in the crowd. Where did all these dancers come from, I wondered?

We formed lines, one behind the other. Famous ballet instructor, Albertina Rasch, showed us dance steps. One line at a time did the steps. I could see there were many excellent dancers. When we finished, they took names, but not mine. However, I was told, "You were good. Don't call us, we'll call you."

When I got back in the car with my mother, I told her, "I'll be dancing in that movie. They said I was good and that they'll call me."

Days passed, and I picked up the receiver many times to make sure the phone worked. Since I hadn't heard, I figured they hadn't started yet. Then another day went by, and no calls. I finally phoned my friend and told her I hadn't heard yet. There was a silence on the other end. She finally told me: "Rehearsals have already started for one of the numbers," then added those famous words, "'Don't call us, we'll call you,' means, forget it. I'm working on another picture or I would have checked with you earlier."

After I hung up, I thought, no, no. This can't be happening. I've got to dance in that movie. I got the studio phone number from a neighbor who worked in one of the departments. I phoned and explained to the person who answered that I was supposed to be in *Rosalie*, but my phone's been out of order. I told her I'd be there that afternoon. Then I pleaded with Mother to make that long drive again.

"This is ridiculous," she said. "It will probably be a wild goose chase."

But she drove me there, and when we got to the gate, I told the guard, "I'm supposed to be with the dancers for *Rosalie*, and I'm late." He let me pass through. When I got to the soundstage, they weren't doing the same steps we did during the first audition. With a hundred girls or more there, nobody seemed to realize I had come back for the second time. But I got into a line while they showed us some simple movements. They took my name and told us that we would go into rehearsal the next week.

I kept telling myself, I'm in! I'm in! I'm in the movies! When I told Mother, I was beside myself with joy. She was amazed that everything had worked out so well for me. But something inside me knew it would.

That night, I told my parents I was taking a professional name, like everyone else. It was something I'd thought about for some time. I had always liked the name Karen, but I would spell mine with a "C." The letter "K" seemed like it should belong to a tall girl—the "C" was more suited to me. My name Aileen came from Mother's favorite actress, Aileen Pringle. Our family name was Morris. I wanted something close, so I chose "Marsh." Caren Marsh. I liked the way it looked, and the way it sounded. My parents liked it too. With that settled, I really felt like I was ready for the movies. All I had to do was remember to tell them about my name change when I returned to the studio.

After rehearsals started, the MGM buses drove us to the back lot to a huge extravagant courtyard scene. Dancers piled out of the buses and were directed to the rehearsal area. The enormity of the whole production amazed me. So this is what it's like to be a dancer in a movie, I thought. My first movie—and I was so excited. Every morning they bussed us from the studio to the back lot where we rehearsed all day and into the night. The dancing part became an easy ritual, moving to the music and doing the different steps we had been taught. They measured and fitted each of us for what would be our gorgeous costumes and heavy headdresses.

I filled out a slip since this was my first job. It had to do with Social Security and the money I'd receive when I was old. Old? I'm only eighteen, I said to myself. Who cares about getting any money when I'm an old woman? Now is when I want to make some money.

I made friends with a few of the girls. They had been in earlier movies and told me about their experiences, which helped.

"Be sure to call Central Casting every day. Call when you're not working so they'll get to know your name and send you out on calls for jobs. They may not all be for dancing, but you can make money as an extra too." Then they added, "Their line is always busy, but just hang up and dial again—then hang up and try again. Sometimes it will take half an hour until you reach them. You just have to keep on trying and eventually you'll get through."

After rehearsing for a week, they told us they'd be shooting the dance sequence at night. When that evening arrived, we dressed in our costumes, ready to dance under the stars. It was all new to me. The bright lights lit up the sky as well as the set. Dew settled on our dance floor. I wondered how the studio could handle all of these dancers and crew, even providing us with hot meals during the break, and if all musicals were made on such a grand scale.

Waiting to shoot was the hardest part for me. They spent a lot of time preparing to line up a shot, then eventually shooting the scene. We danced a little, then waited a lot. That tired me, as time dragged, and my costume got heavier. I thought we'd be dancing all the time, but I quickly learned how tedious it could be to make a movie.

After a long day and night, we had to be there again early the following morning. I think that the exciting part of it all was just thinking about being in a movie. Now that I appeared in one, it didn't seem at all like so much fun. That night, as we worked, I had mixed emotions, experiencing my first film job.

I soon discovered that all the studios now wanted tap dancers—ballet was not as popular as it had been. I'd never tap danced, but I found myself on call for tap dancers at 20th Century-Fox. Nick Castle, the dance director—a man with a lot of talent and style, showed us a few dance steps. I stood in the back row wondering if I could pick them up, but I caught on right away, which surprised me. As I tap danced, I told myself never to say you can't do something. We formed new lines, learned more steps, and I moved up front.

"I'm tapping, I'm tapping," I kept saying to myself.

After the audition, I told Mr. Castle how much I enjoyed learning his steps. But I didn't tell him this was my first attempt.

"You're a really good dancer," he told me. "I'd like to use you in all my future pictures."

I'd heard about ballet being the foundation for any type of dance. They were right. Now I tap danced too.

# Chapter Six

I was working on the MGM lot one day, just after I turned nineteen, when a young man approached me and asked if I'd like to be the stand-in for Judy Garland, one of their new players. They were making *The Wizard of Oz*, and he thought my appearance and my dance ability would be a perfect fit.

"Just what would I be doing as a stand-in?" I asked. As a dancer I never heard of "stand-ins."

"Well, a stand-in takes the place of the actor while they're setting up the shot—the lights, camera—all that. You could be sitting, or standing, or . . . whatever."

"I wouldn't appear in the movie, would I?"

"A stand-in never actually appears in the film but is important for all the technical work that is performed before the shooting. When they are ready for the shoot, they will call for Judy, who will then take your place."

That sounded interesting to me, and I accepted the job. I was sorry now that I hadn't been able to spend any time with Judy when she spent the night at our house with my sister Dorothy. It would have been a nice introduction to our working together.

I arrived at MGM at six in the morning on my first day and went to the makeup department. A guard stopped me at the entrance and asked my name and the production—then checked his list and directed me down a hall past rows of private makeup rooms for the stars and featured players to a large room for bit players and extras. I checked in and observed the bustling activity as many women, beautifully made up for their particular parts, left the room. I figured they must have arrived at five o'clock, or earlier.

I felt self conscious, with my bare face hanging out until I noticed all the other women, young and old, also waiting to be made up. Some looked as though they hadn't awakened yet, with puffy eyes and messy hair. Others sat before brightly lit mirrors, awaiting their makeup. Not knowing just where to go, I stood there for a moment looking bewildered. I hadn't expected a mob scene like this.

One of the makeup men spotted me. As he approached, I said, "Good morning, I'm here for the *Wizard of Oz* production. I'm Judy Garland's stand-in."

"Take a seat over there, darling," he said, pointing to a chair a pretty actress was leaving. "I'll be with you shortly."

I plopped down in a chair and gazed into the mirror framed by a galaxy of lights. A naked face stared back at me. I felt undressed without makeup and hoped I would be next.

In a few minutes he returned and went right to work on me. First, he dipped a sponge into a bowl of water. Then after squeezing out most of the water, he swirled it around on a pancake makeup and applied it to my face. As he smoothed it on, he told me, "This doesn't have a heavy 'theatrical' look that's used for black and white—it's very light and natural for Technicolor."

Next were the eye makeup, rouge, and lipstick. He stood back and admired the results. I looked in the mirror and wondered who that beautiful creature was who looked back at me with that peaches-and-cream complexion. I wanted some of that for every day. "What shade is this?" I asked.

"That's called 4N," he said.

I knew it was a Max Factor product. I never looked better and felt like a movie star. Those makeup men could work wonders. As I left, more bare faces arrived.

The hair department seemed as busy as the makeup department. Some actresses had their hair up in rollers, others were in pin curls, and two or three were having their hair curled with curling irons. Over in one corner, a hairdresser brushed out an actress's long hair, swept it up on top of her head, put a sheer stocking cap over it, and added a short, sexy-looking blonde wig. In minutes, her whole appearance had changed.

Next to her, another actress, with short-cropped, auburn hair, was fitted with a long dark wig that fell to her waist. She didn't look like the same woman. What would they do with my shoulder-length pageboy?

I stood by waiting patiently. Finally, a hairdresser looked my way. I approached her and said, "I'm here for the *Wizard of Oz* production. I'm standing-in for Judy Garland."

She smiled, and said, "Sit over here in this chair. I'll be right with you."

As I waited, I looked around surprised to see how many wigs they used. When she returned, she propped up a photo of Judy Garland, as Dorothy, on the makeup table in front of me. Now how are they going to make me look like that? I looked at the photo showing long pony tails that hung over each shoulder, tied with a ribbon. My hair wasn't that long.

The hairdresser must have guessed my thoughts. "We'll have your hair looking like that in no time," she said, as she held up a hairpiece that must have been fourteen inches long and resembled a pony tail. I watched her in the mirror as she parted my hair down one side in front of my ear, then wrapped that part of my hair around the pony tail and pinned it in place. She repeated the process on the other side. Voila! Like a miracle, my hair looked just like Judy's.

At my next stop, the women's wardrobe department, I saw a lady carrying an armload of costumes on hangers. "Good morning," I said. "I'm here for the *Wizard of Oz* production. I'm Judy Garland's stand-in."

"Just wait over there, honey," she said, pointing to a chair. "I'll be with you as soon as all these other girls are costumed and on their way."

MGM had the most magnificent costumes, including evening gowns of the finest fabrics, jeweled jackets, and an array of beaded gowns, all of them so rich looking. How fortunate I was to be working in the grandest and most important studio in all of Hollywood. Only a studio like MGM could afford the best.

When the wardrobe lady returned, she said, "Your costume is right over here." She led me to a dressing room and there on a rack hung a blue-and-white, checked pinafore and a pale pink, puff-sleeved blouse. I slipped out of my slacks and shirt and put on my costume. I looked in the mirror and saw little Dorothy, all ready to enter the Land of Oz

The wardrobe lady stuck her head in the door and with a look of satisfaction, she said, "Well, I see we don't have to do any adjusting—it fits just fine. Be glad you're not forced to wear a corset like little Judy. Leave your things in the dressing room. Someone will be here to take your costume back when you're through." Then she handed me a pair of socks that matched the blue in the pinafore. "Your shoes will be waiting for you on the set. Better get going now, honey, you don't want to be late."

I hurried off to find the soundstage. The building bustled with activity; electricians moving lights and cables, carpenters hammering, others moving pieces of the set around, and some yelling out orders. As I neared the set, I saw the forest in the background, then the yellow brick road, just as I remembered from the book.

A wardrobe lady approached me with a pair of sparkling red shoes. "Sit over here, honey," she said, "and see if these fit." I tried on the sequin-covered shoes. They glittered in the light—but they were red. I remembered in the book Dorothy wore silver shoes. I asked her about that and she said, "Silver doesn't show up that well in Technicolor. That's why they were changed to red." That sounded reasonable, as I learned a few tricks of the trade. I told her I was a dancer, and all this was new to me.

"Well," she said, "you'll soon be dancing down the yellow brick road."

I bubbled inside just thinking about it. "I'm surprised I'm in a scene with a forest," I said. "What about the cyclone? And Munchkinland, where Dorothy gets her red shoes? How come we start in the forest?"

She smiled, and explained that movies were rarely shot in sequence, and that Munchkinland and the cyclone would be shot sometime later.

I asked her to point out the director and cameraman to me. Artie Miller had told me they were the two most important people on the set.

She pointed to a tall, good-looking man who stood near the camera. "That's the director, Victor Fleming—he's talking to Harold Rosson, the cameraman."

I learned a lot on my first day from that nice wardrobe lady.

After she left, I sat down and waited for something to happen. But people still ran all over the place doing what they had to do. As I waited, I wished I had taken up knitting or brought a book. I asked someone the time—it was almost noon. I had thought as soon as I got to the set, I'd be a stand-in. I was anxious to go to work.

Then somebody yelled, "Ready for Judy's stand-in."

I jumped out of my chair and hurried over to the yellow brick road where Mr. Fleming stood. They placed me at the edge of the forest on the yellow brick road. "Now, stand there. Then let's see you walk down the road from where you are to the end."

As I walked back to my mark, a very pretty girl named Donna joined me. As assistant choreographer on the movie, she demonstrated a sort of skipping dance step to do down the yellow brick road. The steps looked easy, and I soon understood why they chose me, a dancer, for the job. The steps would have been tricky to learn for a non-dancer. After that, I stood in that one spot and waited for further directions.

When the hot lights came on, they held a small object in front of my nose.

"What's that?" I asked.

"It's a light meter, darling."

Well, something new to learn about. All I could say was, "Oh."

So I stood there, hot and tired and waiting while the crew set up the lighting and the camera angles. Those lights threw out a tremendous amount of heat and were hotter and brighter than usual for that new Technicolor film that literally turned the set into daylight. When I danced down the yellow brick road, the hot work quickly became almost unbearable. Even the crew perspired. Finally, they pushed aside the gigantic stage door, turned off the hot lights and turned on the huge fans until we could breathe comfortably again. Production had to wait momentarily. A short time later, they closed the door and production continued. If only we'd had air-conditioning in those days.

When I worked in *Rosalie*, I learned a lot about patience working in "movieland." I thought we all waited because of the huge dance production. But I was wrong. There were long waits on the *Oz* set too. It's all part of the process. It simply takes a lot of time to set up for a scene.

"Okay," the director said. "Let's try this one."

I danced down the road. Then I did it again and again until they were satisfied with the lights and camera, and the distance that had to be covered for the shot.

With everything set up the way they wanted it, they called for Judy, who had been studying with her teacher. When she approached me, we were mirror images in the same outfits, to our braids, and our sparkling red shoes. When they began to film, I stepped out of the scene, and Judy stepped in. They called, "Action!" And off she went down the yellow brick road. From the back, it would have been difficult to tell us apart.

Judy asked me to join her and her teacher in the commissary for lunch. That would be the first of several lunches we would have together.

"Judy, do you remember meeting me briefly two years ago when you were spending the night at our house with my sister, Dorothy Morris, your Bancroft Junior High friend?"

She laughed, "You're her sister? Sure, I remember. You were on your way to a dance class, then after you returned, you were getting ready to go on a date." She told me about the fun she and Dorothy had together, and how she loved playing with our dogs, "Duchess" and "Boy." Then, looking quite pleased, she said, "Do you know, I got to graduate from Bancroft? I'm in the graduating class school picture."

I told her, "Dorothy still has that photo, and she pointed you out to me one time. You were standing at one end of the second row." I could tell the way her eyes lit up that graduating from Bancroft, and being in that 1937 school photo, meant a lot to her.

Lunch was the only opportunity we had to be with each other. When I worked on the set, Judy was busy with her school work. The law stated that as a minor, you had to spend a certain amount of time on your studies. I was glad to have already graduated from Hollywood High and had all that behind me. She amazed me how she could do math, history, geography and other studies, then at a moment's notice, when she heard, "Ready on the set, Judy," she could suddenly turn into Dorothy Gale of Kansas.

Sitting with her at lunch, I felt a bit guilty with my chicken sandwich and chocolate milk, while she only had a bowl of soup. "Damned soup," she mumbled under her breath. We both understood that the camera adds about ten pounds to your appearance on the screen. I heard later that the studio had people watching Judy at lunch to make sure she only had soup. If not, they were to report any infractions to the head office.

At another lunch together, we talked about our cameraman friend, Artie Miller, who worked on her movie *Pigskin Parade* two years earlier. She thought a lot of Artie and was so glad he had asked Dorothy to look her up at school. She added that she hated the way they dressed her in that picture, and when she saw herself on the screen, she couldn't stand the way she looked. As cute as I considered her to be, I had the feeling she thought of herself as being very unattractive. I heard that Judy always wished she could have been as beautiful as Lana Turner. Something a lot of girls wished for.

Judy told me she loved to do watercolors. She said she could lose herself completely when she painted. I wanted to say to her, "Judy, what talents you have. I wonder if you know it."

After our lunches, Judy would leave with her teacher for more school work. I went back to the set. After several days that set folded up, and I waited to be called for the next scene that would be shot in Munchkinland about a month later.

In Munchkinland, I felt as though I was in a little storybook village with cartoon houses and oversized flowers, all very colorful. For a magical moment one day, I stood there where the yellow brick road began and closed my eyes, imagining I was the real Dorothy. How would it feel to live in a world like this? The tiny buildings and narrow streets, the small lagoon with the arched bridge. I was almost small enough to be a Munchkin. Would they let me live here? If I clicked my heels three times, would I be transported back home? Kansas? Hollywood?

One day after a morning of work, I heard the shuffle of tiny feet as the Munchkins returned to the set from lunch. I asked one of the little ladies, "Where do you eat? I never see any of you in the commissary."

"Our lunch is catered to us on the soundstage next door. That's why you never see us," she said.

That answered one question, but I never asked if they had special little tables and chairs for them. Then once again I looked around at the set—the tiny village. It would seem logical for them all to disappear into those little houses for lunch. But this really wasn't Munchkinland. This was Hollywood.

During one of the rehearsals, they handed me Toto, a cute little Cairn terrier. I held her tight as I climbed into a miniature carriage pulled by two Shetland ponies. A Munchkin presented me with a bouquet of flowers, and then I rode around the square and rehearsed the scene, while the hot lights and camera were set up. I looked down at Toto and wondered—is she the star or Toto's stand-in? I couldn't tell the difference. Was I a stand-in carrying a stand-in?

In the next sequence, I stood at the beginning of the yellow brick road, in the center of the square. They told me how far to walk before beginning to skip. Then the skipping turned into the famous dance steps, and off I went, down the yellow brick road with Toto running alongside me. That little dog amazed me. She knew exactly what to do as her trainer signaled to her. That smart and adorable dog seemed to sense how important she was to the movie.

With the Munchkinland sequence finished, production moved to another set a few weeks later. Next, we shot the exterior of the farmhouse. They set up these huge fans aimed at the front of the house. They told me, "Stand outside the gate, darling, while we line up this shot."

When ready to rehearse, the director said to me, "You approach the gate, open it, and head for the front door. We will cut there." Then he warned me, "Now remember, it's a cyclone and the wind machines will be blowing hard, so be prepared."

Next, I heard, "Action!" And the wind blew. I had no idea those machines could blow so hard. I could barely move to the gate. When I did reach the gate, I could hardly open it. I wondered if I could make it to the front door without being blown over. I struggled, but I made it as somebody yelled, "Cut!" At that moment, I was glad to be living in California and not Kansas if they have cyclones like that.

It was bad enough the first time, but then they said they had to do another "take." The problem had something to do with the camera angle. So we did it again. Then a third time and fighting that awful wind tired me. At last they had it right, and I could relax. They called for Judy. I stepped out of the scene, and she stepped in. When they called for "Action," the wind blew, and Judy struggled through a perfect first-take. It pleased me that my job as stand-in, and rehearsing over and over again, made it easier for her.

When rehearsals began on the bedroom scene, I was placed in front of the window looking out at a huge movie screen that showed things flying by: a cow, a chicken coop, rocking chair, bicycle, a tree, and other objects. The camera was at my back and would be shooting past me to the window. I stood on a floor that tilted back and forth. It wasn't easy to keep my balance. Then they changed the scene. Dorothy would not stand at the window looking out—she would sit on the edge of the bed and see it all from there. They scrapped the tilting floor. I was glad for Judy's sake.

Being a stand-in can be tedious, but interesting work, standing in one place for a long time. I watched the crew set up for a scene, adjust the lights, and set the camera angles just right. Then, of course, there were the light meter readings in front of your nose. We didn't have to go through all that at dance rehearsals. Guess I was a dancer at heart.

On the set one morning, I heard that MGM was going to enter a *Wizard of Oz* float in the Pasadena Rose Bowl Parade. Bobbie Koshay, Judy's double, was scheduled to portray Dorothy on the float.

Two days before New Year's Day, I received a phone call from the studio. "Bobbie is ill and won't be able to make it. Be at the studio at six New Year's morning. Go to the makeup department. You are Dorothy on the float."

I was so excited. When I told my family, they were as excited as I was. I phoned all my friends and my family phoned their friends. Everyone planned to drive to Pasadena at four in the morning so they could get a seat on the curb and wave to me as I passed by.

I couldn't sleep on New Year's Eve. Daddy drove me to the studio at five o'clock in the morning so I'd be on time. There were no freeways then. It was still dark when we left, and the drive past all those oil wells pumping and pumping seemed endless. He let me off at the gate. I entered the building that housed the makeup department and was greeted by one of the production assistants.

"Good morning," I said with a smile. "Here I am."

He looked puzzled. "Didn't anyone phone you?"

"Phone me for what?" I asked.

"To tell you that Bobbie felt better and is being made up now."

I couldn't believe it. What was he saying—how could they do this to me?

"Darling, I'm so sorry," he said. "Someone should have called you. We'll send you back home in a car. I'm sorry."

I was so shocked; I shook as I phoned Mother to let her know before they left for Pasadena. She couldn't believe what happened either.

"Daddy's on his way home," I told her. "A studio car will bring me back."

I cried all the way home—the tears wouldn't stop. I was not only disappointed but felt sorry for all my friends who had left two hours earlier to get a place on the curb so they could see me. I was so humiliated. What will they think when Dorothy goes by on that float, and it isn't me? Then there were my parents' friends. Some lived an hour away from Pasadena. How convenient to have had television then.

The driver looked at me in the rearview mirror. "Are you all right?" he asked.

In between sobs, I told him what happened. He was very sympathetic and said two words I'll never forget: "That's showbiz."

I learned a very important lesson that day: I will never again tell anyone what I'm planning to do—until I've done it.

They continued filming that beautiful story, but my part in it was completed. Little did L. Frank Baum know that his book, *The Wizard of Oz*, would be a favorite of young and old alike for decades, and then be made into a motion picture where the legend would continue. I only had a small part in all of it, but it was a part I will never forget. As I look back on my many past performances, *The Wizard of Oz* will always hold a special place in my heart. For a few moments in time, I *was* Dorothy, in the magical Land of Oz *The Wizard of Oz* won two Oscars: one for best musical score, and one for best song, "Over the Rainbow," composed by Harold Arlen and E. Y. "Yip" Harburg. And they presented Judy with a miniature statuette for her outstanding performance as a screen juvenile for that year.

# Chapter Seven

Those girls in *Rosalie* weren't kidding when they told me to keep trying after getting a busy signal from Central Casting. One day, after dialing until my finger hurt, I hadn't gotten through to them yet—it had been over twenty minutes. At last I heard, "Central Casting."

I gave them my name, then waited.

"Report to Selznick International Studios at seven, tomorrow morning," I was told, "You'll be sent to wardrobe, then do a scene in *Gone With the Wind.*"

I'd read the book and loved the story. I wondered what the scene would be. I had just survived a tornado in *Oz*, and now I faced *Gone With the Wind.*

In the Wardrobe Department, a lady helped fit me with pantaloons, a bodice, then a corset that she tightly laced. She slipped a ruffled petticoat over my head, then a dress with tight waist and full skirt. How did ladies of the time dance in all that clothing? Could I even eat lunch bound up like that? I looked in the mirror and marveled at what that corset had done to my already tiny waist.

When we arrived on the set, the director, Victor Fleming, who had directed *The Wizard of Oz*, smiled, and said "Hello." He proceeded to describe the scene we girls would be in. Guests had arrived at Ashley Wilkes' "Twelve Oaks" plantation for a picnic and ball. Ashley, of course, was played by Leslie Howard, who was a favorite of mine. I had seen him in *Of Human Bondage*, with Bette Davis, several years before and was touched by his performance.

To set up the scene, he told us, "You girls are here in the bedroom for your afternoon naps before the ball." He gave directions on where we would be napping and on what beds. We were to remove our dresses, then our petticoats. Our white pantaloons, bodices, and corsets were to remain on for the nap.

During the light and camera set up, we had several rehearsals. Then, "Quiet on the set! Roll 'em. . . . Action."

We struggled to unfasten our dresses and let them drop on the floor and slipped off the ruffled petticoats too. Hattie McDaniel, who played the part of Mammy, picked everything up. We stretched out on the beds for our naps. During one of the rehearsals, I peeked at Scarlett, played by the gorgeous Vivien Leigh, who tiptoed among us.

Someone yelled, "Cut." And the scene was over. We did two more takes before the director was satisfied. It took a whole day to shoot that one scene—and most of it, just waiting around.

So this is "extra" work, I thought. Why was extra work considered at the bottom of the ladder when extras were so important to a scene? What would a picnic scene be like if only the stars were there? How about those movie football games? What if the stands were empty? Or the empty nightclubs or vacant sidewalks? I hadn't thought much about it before, but from then on, I became more aware of what these people added to a scene. I missed dancing, but my first job as an extra was an experience . . . and I was working.

My sister, Dorothy, was now at Hollywood High School. Because of the three-year age difference, we never attended junior high or high school at the same time. When I graduated as a senior, she entered as a freshman. Because she had acted in plays at grammar school and junior high, she joined Mr. Kachel's drama class too. She was determined to be a serious actress.

In her senior year, Mr. Kachel cast her as the romantic lead in the fall play, *Berkeley Square*. She gave an impressive performance, and I was so proud of her. After the show, an agent approached her and wanted to represent her. Our parents met him and recognized him to be an agent with a good reputation.

A week later, Dorothy signed with him and went out on interviews. She soon learned the business was full of rejections. She experienced long periods of no interviews at all. In the meantime, she landed a role in a play at the Pasadena Playhouse. She also enrolled in Maria Ouspenskaya's drama school in Hollywood where she studied the Stanislavsky Method, all this in preparation for the acting career she was determined to have.

The whole year went by before she landed a small part in a Jane Withers movie, *Her First Beau*, which enabled her to get her Screen Actors Guild card.

One day, her agent called and said he had arranged a screen test for her at MGM. She was among many girls testing for the part in an *Andy Hardy* film. The following day, the test director, Fred Wilcox, phoned to say he was sorry she didn't get the role. Dorothy was terribly disappointed because she felt she had given her best. But, he added, "Louis B. Mayer saw your test and said, 'I don't know who that girl is, or what she's done, but sign her up.'"

Happily, my little sister, Dorothy Morris, was now under contract to MGM. She would appear in forty pictures over the next five years and married her high school sweetheart in 1943.

One day, Central Casting sent me to MGM. "Bring a bathing suit—some of you will be required to go into the water."

I reported to the main gate, and they bussed several of us to the lake on the back-lot. The movie, *40 Little Mothers*, starred Eddie Cantor. In between takes one day, as we sat near the lake, I chatted with one of the MGM contract players, and she was adorable. She was the same height as me with a figure like a Petty drawing. Her name was Diana Lewis. She later married William Powell and acquired the nickname "Mousie."

I met another attractive girl with shoulder-length blonde hair by the name of Constance Keane. The following year she signed a contract with Paramount and changed her name to Veronica Lake. She became a famous star, and women all over America copied her peek-a-boo hairstyle.

How interesting to look around the Hollywood scene and try to imagine who might next become a star. One day you would see a handsome young man or beautiful girl walking around the movie lot, and the next thing you knew, they were contract players, some on their way to stardom. All wanted to achieve that goal, but few really made it. One thing was certain to me; Hollywood was full of beautiful people.

One night I came home from a date and told Mother, "You should see him rumba." I was talking about a boyfriend, who turned out to be much more than that. We often danced at the La Conga nightclub on Vine Street. Others moved off the floor just to watch us dance. I said, "He is so darling. I've known him for two years as a friend, and now we love each other. We want to get married."

Mother looked very serious when she responded, "Babe, there's more to marriage than dancing. Daddy and I don't think he's right for you. You're twenty years old, and we can't stop you if that's really what you want. But, remember, you can't rumba your way through life."

I discovered later how true those words were. We married, but four years later we divorced. I moved back to live with my parents.

Another movie —and more dancing. This time it was a Fox musical, *That Night in Rio*, starring Alice Faye and Don Ameche. We worked with Carmen Miranda, the Brazilian Bombshell. It was marvelous the way she moved while balancing that bowl of fruit on her head. She was short, like me, but appeared much taller because of platform sandals that lifted her a good four inches off the floor. I loved it when she danced and rolled her eyes while singing "Chica Chica Boom Chic." I always felt like applauding when she did that number.

Hermes Pan, our dance director, was a wonderful dancer himself and usually worked with Ginger Rogers and Fred Astaire.

Carmen Miranda had her own three-piece combo. I told one of her musicians, "I wish I could dance the samba like they do in Brazil. It looks much more exciting than the way we do it here in the States. I love your style and the way you move your bodies."

He asked, "Would you like to learn? I can show you."

"When?"

"Come on," he said. "There's a corner over here where we won't be in the way."

He took me in his arms in the basic dance position. As we started the familiar steps, I felt him leading the upper part of my body in these large, circular motions like we were glued together. Round and round the floor we went. The samba was always a beautiful dance to watch, and now it was a beautiful feeling. How different from the American version. When we stopped, I stood breathless. "I could dance for hours with a good dancer like you," I said, as they called for dancers back on the set. There's no end to learning.

# Chapter Eight

On Sunday morning, December 7, 1941, I watched my husband and friend play tennis at the country club. But my mind wandered back over the previous two years of married life. I still danced in musicals. Saturday evenings at Ciro's we could be seen leading a conga line around the floor with many of Hollywood's biggest stars following behind. We looked like a great pair, still trying to "rumba our way through life," but things weren't going all that well. Thoughts of separation tumbled through my head, when suddenly over the loudspeaker came a shocking announcement: "Attention! Attention! Pearl Harbor has just been bombed! Repeat! Pearl Harbor has just been bombed!"

We ran into the clubhouse where people were gathered around the radio listening to the news report. Later, President Roosevelt declared war on the Japanese. We were all shocked because none of us ever thought we would be dragged into a war. But this was different. America had been attacked, and suddenly everything changed.

During the next four years, gasoline and food was rationed. We draped black fabric over the curtains at night so no light would filter through. Neighbors volunteered to be air raid wardens—they walked the streets at night to check on darkened windows and to warn us all in the event of an air raid. Boys volunteered to enlist, others were being drafted. Cities conducted air raid drills accompanied by the awful wail of the sirens.

Late one night the sirens screamed and roused us from a sound sleep. We knew we didn't have drills at that late hour. There'd been rumors of enemy submarines hiding in the Pacific off the California coast. Numb with fright, we tried to decide what to do. Hide under the bed? In the closet? What? Eventually, the "all clear" sounded, and in the morning, we heard it had been a false alarm. I could only imagine what it must have been like for our Allies, hearing the wail of the sirens, followed by the bombs. Here, thousands of miles away, we slept safe.

The studios made more musicals because audiences wanted movies that'd help take their minds off the war. I filmed one musical after another at the different studios. In a way, it was sad it took a war to bring me all those jobs.

My husband volunteered for the service and went to Texas for training. For the first time in my life, I lived alone in our Hollywood apartment. It was a life I knew I'd have to get used to since we were on our way to a divorce.

The days I worked on a movie set and waited for the filming to begin, I kept busy knitting sweaters for the servicemen. I tried not to make any mistakes. Who'd end up wearing one of my sweaters, I'd never know, but I wanted them to be perfect.

Ann Lehr, a woman who lived in a large house a few blocks from my apartment, turned her home into a haven for enlisted men. Starlets served breakfast at long tables before the men left for their posts. The boys all adored her for the homey atmosphere and called her "Mom Lehr." When I wasn't working, I walked the few blocks to her home and helped serve meals. Some boys had wives, and some had sweethearts. Others had no family at all. I always hugged them goodbye. Some asked if they could write to me, and I gave them my address and promised to write back.

I joined the Naval Aid Auxiliary and wore a uniform when on

duty. We greeted troop ships as they put in to port from Europe and the South Pacific. They docked at Wilmington Harbor, and we waited for them with hot coffee and donuts. The Army band played as the ship entered the breakwater. Friends and families stood on the dock, waved, and cheered them home. What a touching scene, seeing them meet again after months overseas.

The Hollywood Canteen drew many enlisted men who liked to dance. Famous entertainers and movie stars volunteered their evenings to dance, serve food, entertain or just talk. I saw several stars give the boys the kind of kisses they would never forget. I danced there several evenings a week if I didn't have an early call in the morning. Jitterbugging was popular, and I was happy to dance with these young men who needed a partner. It was sad, though, to think about them on their way overseas to fight a war. Some of them looked so young—I thought they must be very brave.

One night my girlfriend and I took a bus to the Corona Naval Hospital. We went there once a week to the paraplegic ward to talk with those poor paralyzed boys. We visited from bed to bed and tried to make life a bit more bearable for them. The nurses told us that the patients looked forward to our visits.

One Friday night I made arrangements with the hospital to have eight boys who could travel brought to my home for an afternoon barbecue. After they arrived, Daddy put hot dogs on the grill. Mother brought out baked beans, corn on the cob, a large salad, and her special homemade chocolate cake as we sat around the table on our patio. It was wonderful seeing the joy on the faces of those young men. A touch of home meant a lot to them.

On my following visits they were still talking about that wonderful afternoon. I remember one of the boys, paralyzed from the waist down, liked me to hold his hand. He had no family and told me he was in love with me.

The following week I entered the hospital, greeted the boys and headed down the aisle until I came to his bed. He wasn't there. I asked a nurse where they moved him. I'll never forget her words. "He died a few days ago." He was so young and had no family to care about him. I was glad he knew that I cared. That incident reminded me how terrible war could be, and I cried all the way home.

I auditioned for another musical, *My Best Gal*, dancing alongside Jane Withers. I had first seen Jane in a Shirley Temple film, where she played the part of a pudgy little brat in scenes with Shirley. Though she wasn't pretty, she was adorable, with an infectious vitality and personality. Now in her teens, she was very friendly and real—nothing phony about her. Four good-looking boys, The Williams Brothers, sang in the dance number with us. The one they called Andy would go on to much greater fame. During a break in rehearsals one day, director Anthony Mann called me over. He gave me several bits of dialogue to say in the next scene. Now I had the opportunity to be a "bit" player. It occurred to me maybe I'd better enroll in a drama school. As much as I loved dancing, why not add acting to my career?

I danced again in a Roy Rogers Western, *Hands Across the Border*, co-starring Ruth Terry. In one courtyard scene, twenty-four of us girls danced two different numbers. In the first number, we were all in a colorful Spanish dance. The second number had one group of girls who wore gypsy clothes. I appeared in the other group that wore short western costumes and boots. On the set the photographer called me over from the dance line. He wanted to shoot a picture of me with Roy. "Now stand there together," he said, "and Roy put your arm around the little lady and hold her other hand. Now, look into the camera."

And that was it. I had just had my picture taken with Roy Rogers. He was a real gentleman and made me feel so comfortable posing with him. I didn't know until years later just how much coverage that photo and lobby card would receive.

On another movie, *Hit Parade of 1943*, at Republic Studios in the San Fernando Valley, I found myself working again with dance director Nick Castle. Again, Nick came up with one of his very creative dances. We girls and boys danced on large drums with small drums fastened to each hip. We beat each other's drums while dancing. It was a real challenge to our ability as dancers since the surface of the big drums was so confined.

During rehearsals one day, we heard that MGM was holding auditions late that afternoon for dancers who could pass as teenagers for two upcoming movies, *Girl Crazy* and *Best Foot Forward*. Rehearsals were scheduled to begin within the month. As soon as our rehearsals with Nick Castle finished for the day, we dancers raced to our cars and dashed out to MGM in Culver City. We arrived in time for the audition, along with dancers from other studios. We formed the required lines, each of us hoped to be chosen for one, or both, pictures; Then a lucky break. They told me to step forward and took my name. I had the job for both movies. We didn't have to audition for dancing this time. They chose us on the basis of "type."

After finishing at Republic, I appeared at MGM ready to start rehearsals for *Best Foot Forward*, starring Lucille Ball. It had been a hit Broadway musical, and some of the New York cast had been brought out to Hollywood. The story took place at the fictitious Winsocki Military Institute. Lucille Ball played a fading movie actress who had accepted a young cadet's invitation to the senior prom. She goes, hoping the publicity will boost her diminishing popularity. Harry James and his band furnished music for the prom.

Mothers had to be present on the set for the underage dancers. At twenty-four, I always looked much younger.

We enjoyed almost three months of work because *Girl Crazy* would be filmed as soon as this one was completed. A dancer's salary was fifty-five dollars a week. Not a huge amount today, but considering that the rent for my beautiful Hollywood apartment was fifty-five dollars a month, this was good money.

Rehearsals started, and the dances began. While waiting to rehearse a dance number with dance director Chuck Walters, I sat next to a girl I hadn't met before. June Allyson had come to Hollywood from the New York stage production. She didn't look at all the type I imagined being on glittery, glamorous Broadway. Since I'd never been to New York to see a Broadway musical, I'd always fantasized that stage actors were as glamorous as Hollywood movie actors. It surprised me that June wasn't a Broadway beauty.

The first musical number in the movie started with two busloads of girls who arrived at the Winsocki Academy for the Senior Prom. We spilled out of the buses and ran to the entrance of the building where the cadets waited for us on the front steps. The two girls featured in the number were MGM starlet Gloria DeHaven and June Allyson, fresh from her same role in *Best Foot Forward* on Broadway. They sang "Wish I May, Wish I Might," a song written for the show by Hugh Martin and Ralph Blane, who later would compose the famous "The Trolley Song" for the movie *Meet Me in St. Louis*.

Hugh selected five cadets and five girls to each sing a line in the number. I had the lyrics, "I would knock their little eyes out." We sang to the already recorded voices of professional singers known as "voice doubles."

Three years later, I saw Rita Hayworth in the movie *Gilda* with a voice double singing "Put the Blame on Mame," one of the best dubs I'd ever seen. You'd swear Rita, with all her sensuous movements, really sang that song. I learned that many movie stars had their singing voices dubbed with the singers never receiving screen credit—another well-kept dark secret.

After filming the dance number "Barrelhouse, Boogie Woogie and the Blues," a few of us were invited to see the rushes. When

June appeared, she amazed me. She lit up the whole scene with her personality. I thought: that girl is going places. Later, on the set, I told her so. She gave me a hug and a "Gee, thanks."

Nancy Walker, a wonderful comedienne in her role, didn't clown around during breaks. She appeared to be a very serious, sensible person, and I liked her.

Our white gowns, form fitted to the hips, burst into full net skirts that reached the floor. Choreographer Charles Walters, a sweetheart to work for, had us waltz, boogie, and sing with our dubbed voices. Dance director Jack Donohue choreographed the big Winsocki number. I wasn't sixteen anymore but dancing at the Winsocki Senior Prom took me back to my Hollywood High days. I remembered all the boys I'd danced with and their comments, "You're the best dancer here."

Stars usually disappeared into their portable dressing rooms on the set until their next shooting scene. Meanwhile, we dancers sat around in groups, reading, knitting, or playing cards. Time dragged until they called us for the next scene. One time while waiting, tall, beautiful redheaded Lucille Ball stepped out of her dressing room and walked toward me. "Hi, little one," she said. "You remind me so much of a friend I used to have back in New York." Then she asked, "How would you like to cue me on my lines?"

It would be a good half hour before the dancers would be called again, so I said, "I would love to, Miss Ball," and followed her to her dressing room. I had always been curious about what the interior of a portable dressing room was like. When she opened the door, I stepped into a miniature drawing room, an actor's home away from home. She offered me a seat and said, "When you've learned all your lines, they send you the pink pages with the rewrites. Then you have to forget what you've already learned and memorize new ones. Now let's see if I know them." She handed me several pink pages. I looked them over, glad to be a dancer. It was a lot easier to change steps than to have to learn different lines. I cued her, and she had the dialogue down pat.

A few minutes later she looked at me and said, "You ought to go to New York and get in a show. They don't appreciate talent here when it's under their nose. They like to discover talent elsewhere and bring it back to Hollywood, just like they did with the kids from this New York show. Think about it."

She confided to me that being in a Chesterfield ad in 1933 resulted in her getting to Hollywood. Afterward, she became a Goldwyn Girl in an Eddie Cantor movie, *Roman Scandals*. She'd been in many musical films and played a lot of "bit" parts. "Go to New York and get in a show," she repeated.

A knock on the door interrupted us. "Five minutes, Miss Ball."

The makeup man and hairdresser gave her a last minute touch up. I stood.

"Thanks, Miss Ball," I said, as I left her trailer, "I'll always remember this."

She smiled and said, "Just call me Lucy."

# Chapter Nine

When we finished *Best Foot Forward*, we immediately went into rehearsal for *Girl Crazy*, which had been a big hit on Broadway thirteen years earlier. The screen version starred Mickey Rooney and Judy Garland. I had worked in their pictures before: *Babes in Arms* in 1939, *Strike Up the Band* in 1940 and *Babes on Broadway* in 1942. They were fun jobs because Mickey and Judy clowned around with each other off camera, and he'd often have Judy in hysterics with some of his antics.

Judy and I never spent any private time together, and we hadn't lunched together since *The Wizard of Oz* picture made her a star. The unspoken caste systems in those days at the studios remained—stay with your own kind, and every star knew you didn't mingle on the set with those considered below you. I had heard about a star that had been seen with a friend who worked in the editing department. They ate lunch together in the studio commissary one day, and later they called her into the head office and told her never to do that again.

After hearing that, I thought, is this my Hollywood, or Snootyville? Judy always said "Hi" or "Hello" to me, but that was all, and I understood. I also never reminded Mickey of the time he patted my behind up on the mountaintop in *A Midsummer Night's Dream*.

Our director *for Girl Crazy*, Busby Berkeley, was famous for making kaleidoscopic patterns with his dancers called "The Berkeley Top Shot." He perfected this technique in the early thirties at Warner Brothers.

When I was in junior high, I went to the Warner Brothers Theater on Hollywood Boulevard and saw some of his work in movies like *Footlight Parade* and *Golddiggers of 1933*, and was awed by the beautiful patterns formed by the dancers, shot from overhead cameras. He was known in the business as the only director who shot directly above the dancers. He stood on a crane, high up in the air, and shouted directions through a megaphone. I never dreamed that, someday, I would be chosen by Busby Berkeley to be a dancer in several of his films.

Rehearsals continued on a number that reminded me of the conga line in *Strike Up the Band*. We had rehearsed for almost two weeks on that one number to get it just right. When ready, Berkeley shot it in one take. Working with him again in this movie, along with Mickey and Judy, was a joy, and I hated to see it end.

The rumor on the set of *Girl Crazy* concerned Judy and her deep love for Artie Shaw, the famous bandleader. He'd been married twice and dated Judy. Obviously nothing came of it because he eloped with Lana Turner who became his third wife.

To me, it is interesting to note that while I danced in *Best Foot Forward* and *Girl Crazy*, two MGM musicals meant to entertain the public and keep their minds off the war, my sister Dorothy acted in two MGM war pictures, *The Human Comedy* and *Cry Havoc*, to remind us that a war was going on. Hollywood's way, I suppose, of trying to entertain but still keep us focused on reality.

I happily set out to a casting director's office to be interviewed for my first acting job. On the way there, I remembered the time I auditioned for my first dancing job in the movie *Rosalie*. I'd learned a lot about the business from working on that film. As we sat around waiting for the set to be ready, the girls talked about their experiences. One of them mentioned several actresses who had reached stardom by spending time "on their knees."

"What's wrong with praying for a part?" I asked.

They all stared at me in disbelief.

"Are you for real?" one of them asked.

"Well," I said, "haven't any of you ever prayed for a job?"

When they realized I was serious, one of them said, "We'd better educate you, Little Miss Innocent."

Things they said shocked me. Then I recalled that our old family friend, Artie Miller, warned me about casting couches, but he never mentioned what I heard that day from the girls.

So, there I was, looking for this casting office, an independent one, not connected with any studio. I found the building and parked my car. When I entered, there was no receptionist, simply a plaque on the inside door that read, "Casting." I knocked.

"Come in," a man said.

I opened the door and looked into a rather plain room except for an enormous desk. Behind this enormous desk sat a short, middle-aged, bald-headed man. He smiled, introduced himself, and told me to sit in the chair opposite his desk.

"How old are you?" he asked.

I told him nineteen. I was actually twenty-four.

Then he asked if I'd been working long, where was my last job and at what studio. "How tall are you, darling?"

I guessed everyone in the business is called "darling."

Before I could answer, he said, "Stand up."

I put my purse on the chair and stood.

"Come around here to the side of my desk, so I can see your height."

I walked around to the place he pointed for me to stand. He swiveled his chair around to face me. I first noticed that beads of perspiration had formed on his forehead. Then something caught my eye, and I glanced down. His fly was open, and I was immediately aware that this little man was quite well endowed. I thought, if he asks me to get on my knees, I now know it won't be to pray. When it dawned on me what he was after, I began to laugh and couldn't stop.

Furious at my reaction, his face turned the color of a stop light. He jumped up and shouted, "Get out, get out!"

In the process, he banged that delicate part of his anatomy on the edge of the desk. He let out a yell, grabbed his crotch, and sank back into his chair.

I snatched up my purse and ran from the room, still laughing, unable to contain myself. Out in the fresh air, I stopped laughing, and my emotions turned to shock, disappointment and disillusionment. The tears ran down my cheeks. They don't have to tell me, I already know—this is show business.

An actor's agent, a family friend, asked me to join him and his client Spencer Tracy for a drink. He said they had business to discuss, but he wondered if I would like to meet him.

"Spencer Tracy?" Of course. What an opportunity to meet one of my favorite actors. A top star, Academy Award winner, one of our greatest.

We entered Romanoff's restaurant on Rodeo Drive in Beverly Hills. The room, as usual, was filled to the walls with some of Hollywood's VIPs. Mr. Tracy sat in a booth with a drink in his hand. After being introduced, he gave me a nod and a little smile as we joined him.

While the two of them discussed business, I studied Mr. Tracy. He spoke then as he did in films. The sincerity in his voice seemed as natural. Except for an occasional four-letter word that slipped out, he was the Spencer Tracy we all knew.

My friend excused himself to visit the men's room, and that left me alone with Mr. Tracy and a chance to talk. "Mr. Tracy, I'm a dancer at MGM, and I'm now studying acting. I really admire you and marvel at how you don't seem to be acting at all. I know that's the most difficult accomplishment that any actor can achieve."

He didn't respond and that embarrassed me. Why couldn't I have just sat quietly and waited for him to speak first? After all, who am I that this great actor would care what I thought about him anyway? I wanted to crawl under the table.

Minutes, which seemed like hours, later my friend returned. Another awkward half hour or so of business talk passed, while I sat quietly sipping my Coke and feeling utterly humiliated. It came time for us to leave.

Mr. Tracy turned to me and said, "Any time you're on the lot, Caren, when I'm working, feel free to come on the set and watch."

The stars rarely invited visitors on their sets. What a real compliment. What a nice man, and so in the end, I wasn't sorry I spoke to him. Later, I told my friend what I had said to Mr. Tracy, and how he hadn't said a word at the time.

He just chuckled and said, "Oh, that's Spencer. He hates to talk about his acting."

# Chapter Ten

When Paramount Studios was looking for a "sweet-looking-girl-next-door" type, I auditioned. I read some lines, and the director said I was just right for the part in *Pickup Girl* they were about to make.

He explained, "The Armed Forces are very concerned about the venereal diseases our servicemen are getting. They had instructed them not to get involved with cheap-looking girls. The problem is, they don't suspect that nice-looking girls are the cause as well. That's why this film is being made. It's very important to make the boys aware of this. This is an educational film that will be shown to all our servicemen."

This seemed a little out of character for me, but another opportunity to help the war effort.

The young man, who played the role of a corporal with me, Jack Edwards, attended Hollywood High the same time as my sister Dorothy. She had seen him act in several school plays. Paul Kelly, a fine actor who appeared in *Flying Tigers* and *Ziegfeld Girl*, also had a role in some of the later scenes, so we wouldn't be working together.

On the day of the shooting, it was supposed to be a night scene in a train station. I was to have missed my train and had a long wait.

The corporal approached me and said, "No use waiting here," and picks me up to go dancing and then spend the evening together.

In the next scene was a nightclub, where we danced and drank. When I went to the ladies room, he thinks aloud, "She's a nice, clean kid. There won't be any problem."

My last scene took place in a park, later that same night. We sat on a bench and talked. Then we kissed. We walked through the park as the scene faded.

My two days of work completed, I became eager to view the rushes. I wanted to know how my performance went. The director told me I could only see my scenes. The rest of the film showed what happened to the corporal after he's contacted a disease from that, "nice clean kid." I watched my scenes, pleased with my acting.

Then he told me, "You have to leave now, darling."

I figured this was all part of doing what I could for my country. Of course, I still knitted sweaters for the boys and served them breakfast at Mom Lehr's.

Since I hadn't been to the Hollywood Canteen for several months, I decided to go. The floor was jammed with servicemen and starlets. A young private, a good dancer, asked me to dance.

Then he asked, "Didn't I dance with you a couple of nights ago?"

"No, I wasn't here," I said. We continued dancing while he studied my face.

"You sure look familiar," he said, then abruptly let go of me and said, "I've gotta' get a drink."

He never came back. Later, there he was dancing with someone else. How rude, I thought. Minutes later I danced with another soldier.

Things were going fine until he said, "You sure look familiar."

Funny, that's what the other one said.

He said, "Bye," and left.

I couldn't help but wonder—what's going on here? I'm a good dancer, used a mouthwash, I smell nice. Is it them, or me? Then a corporal approached me.

"How about a dance?" he asked.

"Sure, I'd love to."

Would he react the same as the others?

We danced for a minute when he said, "You sure look familiar."

Oh boy, here we go again.

Then he said, "Hey, weren't you in that training film?"

"Yes, I was," I said. "I did it for my country."

"Hey," he said, "You don't have to be on the defensive about it. Your acting was so good, and you were so believable, I wouldn't think any of the guys would want anything to do with you."

So that was it. The fellows thought I really had something they didn't want, that's why they disappeared so fast. The corporal laughed when I told him what had happened with the others. I must have given an Academy Award performance.

Later, there was an item in the *Daily Variety* that mentioned I'd been seen by more servicemen than any other actress in Hollywood.

The husband-and-wife team of Harry Hayden and Lela Bliss ran the Bliss-Hayden Little Theater in Hollywood. He was a plump little man who'd had small roles in various movies. She was tall and attractive. Their school showcased the best acting in town, and talent scouts always sat in the audience hoping to spot new star material for their studios. At the time, I was cast in the play, *Janie*, which had been on Broadway in 1942. Four girls played Janie, for a week each. Harry directed us, and he and Lela usually had parts in the plays they produced.

At one of the performances, a Warner Brothers scout saw me.

After the show, he said he liked my bubbly personality in the role. "I'm sending you out on an interview and audition with our casting director." He set a date and time.

When I arrived for the audition, they handed me lines nothing like the character I portrayed in *Janie*. It was a heavy, tearjerker. I gave it a try, but they didn't have to tell me I wasn't right for the part.

Once again I found myself in another western costume, only this time I didn't dance. In this Western, I acted opposite cowboy actor Bob Steele, who I had never met. But I liked him immediately the first time he walked up to me, smiled, and said "Hi." His warm smile and friendly eyes won me over. He wasn't a tall man, but strong and well-built. Since I'm barely five feet tall, we made a good pair.

They filmed most of the movie, *The Navajo Kid*, on location at the Iverson Movie Ranch in the San Fernando Valley, near Chatsworth. Over time, hundreds of cowboys and Indians had raced through that area in various Westerns.

In my first scene, I traveled down a bumpy dirt road holding the reins of what I thought was a wagon. Before the shot, I told Bob I was afraid that the wobbly wagon wheels would fly off any moment. He assured me that I was safe and with a smile added, "Caren, you're not in a wagon, you're driving a buckboard." Always something new to learn.

I had several scenes with Bob in which I was coaxing him to come to my birthday party. Other scenes featured him with his sidekick, Sid Saylor. It amazed me how Bob could take a running leap and land on the back of his horse, Coco, a beautiful animal with a blonde mane and tail. Off he would go, galloping into the hills to battle the bad guys. Just like sitting in a movie theater on a Saturday afternoon with the kids stomping and yelling for their hero

Unlike the major studios, which could afford dozens of takes, we shot ours in one. Seldom did you get a second chance. As a result, they shot a Western like this in a fraction of the time. I acted for a change, and it was nice to realize I could both dance and act, and be recognized for my efforts.

A review I received from a critic after shooting *Secrets of a Sorority Girl* encouraged me: "Caren Marsh is another bright-faced and talented young lady who ought to have the major studios clamoring for her work and looks."

I had been divorced for some time. The war ended. When one of my boyfriends picked me up one Sunday for a ride in the country, it surprised me to see him drive up in a brand-new Cadillac.

"When did you get this beautiful car?"

"A few weeks ago. I didn't tell you, I wanted it to be a surprise."

It must have taken him a long time to earn the money for this expensive car. A Cadillac like that cost around $3,000, a small fortune in those days. We pulled into a gas station and talked while the attendant filled the tank, looked under the hood at the water and oil, checked the tires, then cleaned all the windows.

When he was finished, he said, "That will be $1.80." Expensive gas, but it was well worth it for a nice drive in the country. Today, this would be a fairy tale. Back then, it was for real.

In another acting job, if you could call it that, I was supposed to be an expectant mother, lying in a hospital bed, looking terrible, and in pain. The director told me the night before, "Don't get any sleep. We want you to look tired, with bags under your eyes."

There was no need to tell me. I couldn't sleep anyway knowing I'd be acting with Bing Crosby. So I did this scene with no makeup and pretended to be miserable with the camera in my face. Bing sat beside the bed and consoled me. I didn't have any lines, just had to lie there. Later, the set photographer snapped a picture of us sitting together. Bing looked good. I didn't. The movie was *Welcome Stranger*.

I ate lunch with a friend in a restaurant one day, when a woman came to our table and introduced herself as a member of the Women's National Aeronautical Association. She said she'd been watching me and wondered if I'd consider being a contestant, representing her association in a contest. The winner would be Miss Sky Lady of 1947.

"What would I have to do? What kind of contest is it?" I asked.

"You don't have to do anything. Just be yourself. It's a personality contest."

"Thanks for asking," I said, "but I've never entered a contest before. I'm afraid I wouldn't be winning this one for you—so, no thanks."

"The prize is free flying lessons for the winner," she said, to sweeten the pot.

"Did you say, 'Free flying lessons?'"

"Yes, you could learn to fly an airplane."

That was the hook. "Yes, I'd be happy to be your contestant," I said.

I told my friend, "I'm going to be a pilot! I'm going to be a pilot!"

Five other girls appeared in the contest, all of whom represented different organizations. Much to my surprise, I won. My picture was taken standing on the wing of a plane. Later, they presented me with a model of the Ercoupe I'd be flying. Written on the wings were the words, Miss Sky Lady. And on the tail: 1947.

It was a beautiful Saturday morning when I made the two-hour drive to the airport. When I arrived, my smiling instructor congratulated me, then walked with me out to the aircraft parking ramp. There sat the most beautiful little plane I'd ever seen, all silver and shiny. I was ready to go.

"This plane is called an Ercoupe," he said. "Come on, I'll help you up." After I climbed in, he fastened my seat belt and sat beside me. There were two wheels in front of us. "Dual controls," he explained. "One for each of us." Since I had only been a passenger in a plane once before, this was all pretty new to me.

He started the engine, and we taxied out to the runway. "Now I want you to watch carefully. You'll notice the wheel is like the one you have in your car. That's what controls the plane. It's not difficult but will take some patience and practice."

When we were cleared for take-off, he pushed the throttle forward and off we went. After several hundred feet, we lifted gently off the ground—I watched the runway drop away. As we gained altitude, I leaned over the side and looked at the toy city below us. What a wonderful feeling being up there in the blue sky with little clouds floating by.

"Now that you've had a chance to enjoy the scenery, I want you to pay attention to your first lesson."

I watched him as he slowly pulled the wheel toward him, and we gained altitude. When he pushed the wheel forward, the nose went down, and we lost altitude. I followed him through on the controls while we banked to the right, and to the left. This is so easy. I could hardly wait to fly solo and be up there all by myself.

After several simple maneuvers, we entered the traffic pattern and prepared for a landing. We touched down on the runway, taxied to the ramp, and parked. He shut off the engine and gave me additional instructions on the instruments and other items I would have to be familiar with. With that lesson over, we planned to meet again the following Saturday.

On the drive home, I recalled my first time in a plane, over two years earlier. Friends from the east had flown their private plane to Hollywood. They invited me to fly with them to Las Vegas to see a new hotel that was being built. I accepted, and when we arrived at the hotel, a good-looking gentleman with very blue eyes, named Ben Siegel, greeted us. He showed us through the partially built hotel and grounds and told us how it would look when completed. Mr. Siegel couldn't have been more gracious. Both he and his new Flamingo Hotel impressed me.

Flying back to Hollywood, the five of us discussed Mr. Siegel and his hotel. The names Ben and "Bugsy" were often mentioned. The only Bugsy I'd ever heard of was the mobster. Could there be more than one man with that funny name?

I asked. "Who is this Bugsy, you're talking about?"

"You just met him. Ben Siegel—Bugsy Siegel."

I found it hard to believe. That nice looking charming man with the beautiful blue eyes was Bugsy, the mobster? I couldn't wait to get home and tell Mother and Daddy their daughter had spent the afternoon with a mobster.

I later read someone murdered him in his girlfriend's Beverly Hills home. The graphic newspaper photos were horrible.

No, I'll never forget my first plane ride, and I'll always associate it with meeting Bugsy.

I pulled into our driveway, my thoughts once again on my first flying lesson, and the ensuing ones that would lead up to my solo flight.

After several more lessons, I began to feel comfortable, and my instructor felt I was ready to solo.

"Next Saturday will be the day," he said, as we climbed out of the little Ercoupe. When that Saturday arrived, I was very excited and terribly nervous. Although I'd been looking forward to this moment, was I up to it? Can I do it? I'd be up there all alone. It wasn't like my car. I couldn't just stop and get out. What if I forgot how to land? There would be no instructor to take over if I goofed. All those scary thoughts nagged me, but I didn't tell my instructor.

Came the time to get in and get flying. My instructor climbed in and said, "Caren, we'll take her up, fly the pattern, then land. We'll do that until you feel confident enough to go up by yourself.

So we started up, taxied out, and took off. We shot a couple of landings, then he asked, "Do you think you can do it now?"

"One more time," I told him. We took off again—flew the pattern—then landed.

"Okay, I'm ready."

My instructor stepped out—the engine still running. "Up you go, Caren. You can do it," he shouted over the engine noise.

I yelled back, "Up I go," as I pushed the throttle and roared down the runway. In moments I was airborne and tried to concentrate on everything I'd been taught. As I flew the pattern, I pretended my instructor still sat beside me so I wouldn't panic. I talked to him while setting up for a landing. I headed for the end of the runway and kept saying out loud, "Make it s-m-o-o-o-th."

The runway rose to meet me. I touched down with a few bumps and sat the plane on the ground. I had soloed. I taxied over to where my instructor waited for me.

"Beautiful," he said, "now take her up again."

I had gained confidence. This was fun. I knew the thrill of flying—all by myself. I finally understood what pilots have always known—the thrill of being up there in the blue sky with the birds, and the clouds, freedom from the world below. All my negative thoughts vanished. I had wanted to do this, and I did. Something inside told me all the time that I could.

# Chapter Eleven

As any wannabe starlet knows, getting your name and "head-shot" in front of the right people is a highly competitive proposition. You've got to be creative if you want to stand out from the crowd. So now, being a pilot, I seized upon a very unique idea to get more attention.

In the process, "Little Miss Innocent" almost got arrested.

I printed up six thousand leaflets with a photo of me in my Ercoupe and a simple message asking for a contract. Now with the means to see these properly distributed, the gears were set in motion. My instructor had been letting me take the plane up for short flights. The flight this day would not be short. I would follow the roads, find the studios, and throw out the leaflets. I would return to the airport the same way and hopefully no one there would ever know.

My route planned, I settled in the Ercoupe, pushed the throttle in and sped down the runway. Once in the air, I headed for MGM, following the familiar road below. I flew over the studio low enough so I could make sure of hitting my target. Leaflets away! A thousand fluttered down onto the back-lot. People looked up, and I waved to them. Then I headed for Melrose Avenue—it would lead me to RKO and Paramount. Minutes later more leaflets found their marks. Then it was on to the San Fernando Valley and Warner Brothers—another batch over the side. I didn't miss Universal or Republic either. What a sight to see . . . pictures and bios of me gaily flying through the air and surely soon to be in the hands of every prominent movie producer in Hollywood. How brilliant of me! With mission accomplished, I returned to base.

I identified the roads that would lead me back and followed the cars below. With the airport in sight, I made my approach and landed, but I didn't quite return a heroine. After landing, and before I could unfasten my seat belt, my instructor ran out to meet me. "Caren, for cryin' out loud, what have you done? Your plane has been reported flying low over the studios. What the hell made you do that? Do you want to get us all in trouble?"

I confessed to being on an unauthorized mission and showed him some leftover leaflets.

"Caren," he said, breaking into a smile, "you are the limit. I hope this pays off for you, but don't ever do anything like that again."

I had taken a chance and knew it. As I drove up to my house, two police cars were parked at the curb, and two policemen stood out front talking with my mother. I pulled into the driveway, and they came over to my car.

Mother appeared very upset. "These policemen came to the door awhile ago," she said, "and I thought something terrible had happened to you when they asked if you were my daughter. Then they told me what you had done. What made you do that, Babe? You could have killed yourself, or someone else."

"We've got a warrant for your arrest," said one of the officers. "The studios reported you to us. We called the airport and were told that's where your plane had taken off from."

As you might expect, I shook, frightened that I might be carted off to jail, and timidly asked, "What exactly am I being charged with?"

"Littering. It's against the law to litter in public places."

I had to think a moment about that. "Did you say, 'public places?' If they're public places, why don't they open their big gates and let the public in?" I asked.

The policemen looked at each other. I showed them one of my leaflets.

"Don't ever try that again, little lady," one of them said, "or you'll really be in trouble." Then he smiled. "Good luck."

I thanked the officers, and turned to my mother. "I didn't tell you my plan because I knew you'd talk me out of it. I'm sorry you were worried." But I wasn't sorry I'd been gutsy enough to do it!

Today, of course, if any starlet tried to do what I did, she'd probably be instantly surrounded by Air Force fighters or blown out of the sky.

My leaflet attack on the studios led to an article in Jimmy Starr's column in the *Los Angeles Herald-Express*. Republic Studio's casting director read the story and called me in.

He said, "A little girl like you, pulling such a stunt?" He laughed, "Well, since you didn't go down in flames, how would you like a job in *Macbeth*? You will be one of the Ladies in Waiting to Lady Macbeth. We're shooting the movie starring Orson Welles."

What an opportunity, to be in a movie with this great actor.

One afternoon on the set during a break in rehearsal, Mr. Welles beckoned me over. Someone had told him I had dropped leaflets on the studios that fateful day. "Was it true?" he asked.

"Yes," I replied. After that, every time he glanced in my direction, he had a sly grin on his face.

Another day and another movie. This time they cast me in *Adventures of Don Juan*, which starred Errol Flynn. They fitted me with a peasant girl costume. The scene was a Spanish Inn. Don Juan entered with his servant, Laporella, played by character actor, Alan Hale. After Don Juan is seated at the table, he is surrounded by girls who crowd around him.

Director Vincent Sherman placed us for the shot. He picked me to sit directly across the table from our hero. "Now lean forward, toward him."

I looked across the table into the eyes of Errol Flynn, one handsome man. As he looked into my eyes, I could see why he had a reputation for being a Don Juan in real life. Several rehearsals later, the camera rolled, and we shot the scene.

Afterwards, one of his friends came over to me and said, "Mr. Flynn is having a party at his home tomorrow night, and he'd like you to come."

I had heard about those parties he had given in the past, and it was widely known they were on the wild side. Here was my chance to see if it was true about that mirrored ceiling in the guest bedroom—was it really a two-way mirror? Rumor had it that he would sneak a few friends up into the attic to peer down into the bedroom below to watch the antics of the other guests. I wanted to watch too.

But that little inner voice said: "Don't go."

"Why not?"

"It's not your scene."

"But I'm curious."

"You might be sorry the next day."

"Why do I always listen to you?"

"Because you know I'm right."

So I told his friend, "Thank Mr. Flynn for the invitation, but I already have plans for tomorrow night." Dammit!

Producers for a Broadway show came to Hollywood looking for a young girl to play the ingénue in *Strange Bedfellows*. I auditioned, read some lines, and got the role. It sounded exciting since I'd be going to New York. I remembered what Lucille Ball had told me four years earlier: go to New York, get in a show. Now was my chance, and it came to me right here in my hometown.

They told me my salary would be one hundred dollars a week, almost double what I had been earning. When I told my parents about it, Daddy said, "Babe, you can't live in New York on that salary. There's lodging, food, and transportation, besides all the incidentals. I know this is important to you, but I think you'd better turn it down. What if it isn't a hit? What would you do then?"

I told them, "I really want to be in this show. It's a chance to see more than Hollywood, and I'd be on the Broadway stage." Could I really live on that salary in New York? I liked my creature comforts too much to hole up in some dump. Many actors had done just that before they got their break. I lost a lot of sleep thinking about it. Eventually, I took Daddy's advice. I heard later it was a hit show. I wondered what my future might have been if I had accepted the role.

Because I played the "sweet young thing" in that Army training film, *Pickup Girl*, at Paramount they hired me to be a 4-H girl in *Wild Harvest*, directed by Tay Garnett. They thought I would be perfect for the part. From a girl with venereal disease to a healthy and wholesome farm girl—how's *that* for typecasting?

They cast me in a scene with some wonderful actors: Alan Ladd, a Paramount star I had seen in *This Gun for Hire*; Robert Preston, who I would see later in the Broadway musical, *The Music Man*; Lloyd Nolan, who played many roles, but I remember him mostly in *A Tree Grows in Brooklyn*; Allen Jenkins, who played many smalltime gangster roles; and Richard Erdman, who played my new husband in the film. I signed for three days' work. Alan Ladd's character in the film tells me that I can't accompany my husband on their next job, harvesting wheat. I'm the sad little 4-H girl, Natalie, who is disappointed at the news and would have to return home. I only had a few lines to say to Alan Ladd, but I was thrilled to be working with that fine cast.

The fact that I was raised in Hollywood, had never been on a farm in my life, and still got the part—was the "hook" the publicity department used. They took me to a farm, shot photos of me milking cows, running with goats, feeding horses, and even holding a fidgety duck. The pictures appeared in newspapers all over the country and as far away as Hungary. I received unbelievable publicity from this small role.

Paramount Studios called. *Life* wanted to do a layout on the Hollywood actress who had never been on a farm, yet was cast as a 4-H girl. On the appointed day, a photographer arrived at my home and took several photos of me. We drove to Paramount where they shot more pictures with Alan Ladd.

Someone from the publicity department suggested, "Why not take her over to the set of *I Walk Alone,* for some additional shots? Put her in a scene with Burt Lancaster. Did they say Burt Lancaster? That handsome hunk I saw in *The Killers?*

When we arrived on the set, they weren't shooting his scenes that day. I was introduced to another actor they called Kirk who was working in a nightclub scene. I was so disappointed that I wouldn't be photographed with Burt Lancaster. Here was my one chance— and where was he?

"Seat her at a table," someone said, "and have her looking up at Kirk." I posed looking up at this actor who wasn't Burt Lancaster. In the background was actress Lizabeth Scott seated at a piano. When that shot was over, they took two more pictures of us. In one, Kirk is pouring chocolate milk for me while I am sitting on the camera boom, and the other we are standing side by side looking at each other.

Kirk was friendly and easy to like. He told me he had made a few movies before this one, but I'd never heard of him until today. When he was called for his scene, I stayed and watched. I'd never asked an actor for an autographed photo before, but I thought, this man is good looking, has charisma and talent, and I'll bet he'll be a big star someday—ask him for his autograph now. Sure enough, the following year, *Champion* made Kirk Douglas a star and earned him an Academy Award nomination.

I still have his photo where he'd written: "Dear Caren, may all your dreams come true—but more important—may you find happiness when they do. Sincerely, Kirk."

We finished that afternoon, and I went home. The photographer called the next afternoon. "The magazine was pleased with yesterday's shots, and I want you to know that the one of you in your red-and-white striped sweater is being considered for the cover."

I was thrilled at the idea of being on the cover of *Life*. It didn't happen often that a story inside landed on the cover. It was difficult to keep quiet about this possibility to my friends, but I hadn't forgotten the Rose Bowl Parade and my decision not to say anything until something actually happened.

It was a good thing I kept quiet. When that issue appeared on the stands, my picture was not on the cover. I anxiously flipped through the pages, and the 4-H story wasn't there either. I went carefully through the pages once more and found nothing. Later they told me they came up with a story considered more important than a 4-H girl. They said it might appear in a later issue. It never did. Another disappointment to chalk up to the old cliché: "That's showbiz."

Universal Studios was preparing to shoot *Mr. Peabody and the Mermaid*, with William Powell. Another actress and I tested for the part of the mermaid. I heard on the set that Ann Blyth was also being considered. Ann Blyth? That's tough competition, she's a great actress. She had been nominated for an Academy Award for her performance in *Mildred Pierce* several years back. Why would they be testing this other girl and me?

When the time came, I was told to wear a two-piece bathing

suit. On the set, the director motioned me to walk toward the camera. He said, "Now, duck down behind those large rocks in the foreground. Now peek around from behind them and look directly into the camera."

I did as instructed.

"That's right," he said, and after two takes he looked pleased.

But something inside me said the three of us were the same type, so why were they fooling around with this other actress and me? I knew Ann would get the part. And she did.

I was called, "cute" as far back as I can remember. I didn't want to be cute. I wanted to be sexy, like when I played the part of the Red Menace in the Hollywood High School play.

Finally, a part for a sexy girl came up in a movie. To insure my chances of getting the role, I wore a slim, black skirt and tight sweater. Underneath the sweater I stuffed "Falsies" to enhance my 34B bra into a D cup. Before leaving for the interview, I glanced in the mirror with approval. Though barely five feet tall, I now had the figure of a diminutive Jane Russell, one of the "busty" Hollywood beauties—and that's sexy!

I arrived for the interview, and was ushered in to see the casting director who sat behind a large desk. I thought I looked sexy enough to get the part. He looked me over and smiled. "Darling, you sure have the body, but your face is so sweet looking. I'm afraid you wouldn't be right for the part." He added, "I'll tell you what, when something does come up for a cute-looking girl, we'll give you a call."

So there it was again—"cute." And all I wanted was to be sexy. I heard later that Gloria Grahame, who I had seen in *It's a Wonderful Life* and *Crossfire*, got the part.

An actor friend of mine and I had dinner one Friday night at a popular Sunset Boulevard restaurant. A tall, good-looking gentleman approached, who knew my friend. He introduced himself to me as a producer.

The following Saturday morning, this gentleman called and said I'd be perfect to play Jackie Cooper's girlfriend in a show he was producing. They had another actress lined up, but felt she wasn't quite right for the part. The show was to tour across the country, and open in New York for a salary of one hundred dollars a week. He needed my decision right away—rehearsals started in two days at the Masonic Temple on Hollywood Boulevard. My head churned. Touring with a show? Opening in New York? A hundred a week? That was the same salary I had turned down on a previous show. I'd never been out of Hollywood, and here I'd be traveling all over the country. A lot to consider—in a hurry. I told the producer I'd need a minute to think about it, and would he please call back in fifteen minutes?

I hung up the phone and turned to Mother and Daddy. I told them of the offer and sought their opinion. They remembered how they had discouraged me the last time I had a similar opportunity. And they knew how much this would mean to me. But the salary and my surviving in New York still concerned them.

"You don't know anything about this producer, or this show," my parents said. "We want to be sure you know what you're getting yourself into."

The phone rang and I picked it up. "Yes," I told him. "I'd love to be in your show, but you know how parents are. They'd like to meet you first. I've never been out of my hometown Hollywood before."

"No problem," he said, and asked for my address. He also wanted to know if I was an Equity member as well as the Screen Actors Guild.

"Just SAG," I told him.

He invited me to lunch so I could meet his co-producer and arrange for an Equity card, all in one afternoon. When he arrived, my parents were impressed. He was a real gentleman and assured them I would be well taken care of.

I didn't know what to expect, working with Jackie Cooper who had been a popular child star and nominated for an Academy Award for his performance in *Skippy*. The year following, he had the audience weeping in *The Champ*, with Wallace Beery. Would he be temperamental? Spoiled? Difficult? After the first rehearsal, I found him to be friendly and easy to work with.

Once again, remembering my Rose Bowl Parade disappointment nine years before, I decided not to tell my friends about this until we left for the opening performance.

After weeks of rehearsal, we held a one night performance in Oakland, California, to good reviews. Mother and Daddy attended the opening.

From Oakland, we went to Seattle, Washington. *The Seattle Times* said we had a hit and mentioned that, "Caren Marsh is an 'Elfin' brunette for whom the sadly overworked 'cute' is exactly appropriate." Another paper panned the show but was good to me: "Little Caren Marsh is as cute as a button as Jackie Cooper's girlfriend."

As we traveled through various cities, some reviews were better than others. It wasn't until I was on that tour that I noticed, unlike Hollywood, there were very few beautiful girls in these towns. There were pretty ones, here and there, but not the beauties I had seen in my hometown. While growing up in Hollywood, I never thought much about all these gorgeous girls, and the handsome boys. The exceptionally attractive people worked everywhere: behind the counters whipping up sodas, waiting on tables, bus boys, gas station attendants, salesgirls, and extras in the movies.

It had taken my first time out of Hollywood, at the age of twenty-nine, to figure out why my hometown was so filled with these beautiful people. They migrated from all those cities and towns. Some may have won beauty contests or been seen in a school play and encouraged by friends to "go to Hollywood and get in the movies." I simply accepted the notion that beautiful people were abundant everywhere in America.

Most wannabe movie stars found that, after arriving in "Tinsel Town," and struggling for awhile with money running out, they had to take menial jobs to survive. Some, however, kept fighting the odds, with few making it to stardom. Thanks to the tour I was on, I began to realize that growing up in Hollywood had given me a distorted view of real life and people in America.

## Chapter Twelve

In Chicago, we opened at the well-known Blackstone Theater for a longer stay. Newspaper interviews, publicity photos, and the usual parties filled our hours off stage. On opening night, the audience laughter made us feel good. We were getting close to New York—Broadway here we come. But when the reviews came out, they were devastating. They were so bad the show died. There would be no New York opening. Ashton Stevens, the most important Chicago critic, wrote the worst review. Yet he mentioned, "That talented little Caren Marsh is sure to go places."

I phoned my parents and told them the disappointing news. Then I read them my reviews. "I want to go to New York anyway," I told them. "That critic said I was going places, and I feel that place is New York." I also mentioned that my Hollywood agent had an office in New York, and I would contact him when I arrived. They didn't like the idea, but after all, I was now twenty-nine years old and knew the ways of the world. Reluctantly, they wished me the best, adding, "Be sure and let us know how you're doing."

Some of the cast returned to California, others like me continued on to the big city hoping for a break.

Jackie Cooper wanted to be a serious actor and didn't return to

Hollywood. We didn't know then that he would become a successful Broadway actor.

Those of us continuing on caught the train for New York. I stayed awake most of the night pondering my future.

We arrived early in the morning, and I contacted my agent's office, first thing. They arranged for me to stay at a hotel for $5.50 a day. Later I moved to a tiny hotel room for thirty dollars a week. Some of the dancers I met had their meals at Horn and Hardart's automat. They taught me how to make synthetic tomato soup by simply adding ketchup to a cup of hot water. The soda crackers were free. On occasion, I was fortunate to be invited out to dinner in nice restaurants. I realized I had to get a job soon.

I happened to see the Williams Brothers again in New York. We recalled working on a Jane Withers' movie together several years before. Now in the big time, they had a successful nightclub act with Kay Thompson. All the boys were as nice as always, and Andy Williams, the youngest, became a huge singing star known all over the world.

I met a very nice fellow, Russell Arms, a handsome boy with a beautiful voice who also looked for a break. One night we decided to get some Chinese food and have dinner in his small, walk-up apartment. We talked about the theater and our ambitions. He later got his big chance singing for the popular television show, *Your Hit Parade*.

Plenty of "wolves" roamed New York. I thought I had heard most of the lines in Hollywood but learned a few original ones. Let me quote a few:

Producer: "If you want to have sex, don't have it with these boys you meet. You come to me. I'm experienced, and I won't talk about it afterwards."

Actor: "What are you knocking yourself out for, working on a show? You've got a fortune there between your pretty legs."

Producer: "When you're through for the day, let me take you to dinner. Afterwards, we can go back to my penthouse for a nightcap. If you spend the night in bed with me, I promise not to touch you."

It was refreshing to go on a date with a nice guy like Dick Williams, Andy's brother.

The show I turned down still played on Broadway. I saw the matinee, and there she stood, the girl playing the part I could have had for a hundred dollars a week.

I saw several other matinees. One of them, *A Streetcar Named Desire*, with Marlon Brando, Jessica Tandy, Kim Hunter and Karl Malden, was amazing. The scene where Stanley Kowalski stands there with his back to the audience and shouts for his wife, S-T-E-L-L-A!, really blew me away. I'd never reacted like that to any actor's performance in a movie. It took live theatre to leave me shaken for days. I was in awe, and amazed that it could affect me like that. The play won the Pulitzer Prize and the Drama Circle award. I think it was then that I understood that the stage was a most rewarding experience for the actor as well as the audience.

I had heard that the musical, *Heaven on Earth*, featuring Peter Lind Hayes, was holding auditions for singers and dancers. A girl, who had been in several shows, told me, "You'll have a better chance if you can sing as well as dance."

I could carry a tune, but I wasn't a singer. However, I was determined to get in that show, so I started taking singing lessons from a highly recommended coach. Someone told me, "If you have any voice at all, you'll be good enough to audition after his coaching."

The day of the audition, I sang and I danced. Big surprise. I wouldn't be singing or dancing. They cast me as the twelve-year-old daughter of comic Irwin Corey. So, there I was, in my first Broadway musical, acting the part of a child named Fanny Frobisher. From the Red Menace to this!

After three weeks of rehearsals, we boarded a train for Boston tryouts, and then returned to New York for the opening. We all did our best, but got poor reviews. The show lasted a couple of weeks, then closed. Everybody jobless again—but as they say—"That's showbiz."

Since I'd heard so much about Radio City Music Hall, I made the pilgrimage to Rockefeller Center to see the famous Rockettes. After purchasing my ticket, I entered the theater where there was another line waiting for the doors to open to the seating area. While standing in this huge magnificent foyer, I asked a nearby usher how many people the theater could seat.

"Over six thousand," he replied.

I told him I was from California, and this was my first time in New York.

He smiled, and proudly told me, "We have the largest foyer, the largest screen, and the largest theater organ of any movie house in the world. And the stage can be raised and lowered."

Grauman's Chinese Theater on Hollywood Boulevard had always been my idea of the most beautiful theater there ever could be. I loved the colorful murals on the walls and the ornate ceiling, and sinking down in those comfortable seats waiting for the stage show and movie to begin. But I had to admit, Radio City Music Hall did have the biggest of everything.

As the line inched forward, I thanked the usher for the information and entered the theater. I found a seat I liked and got comfortable, as organ music played. I gazed up at the magnificent ceiling, thinking that if I hadn't been there that day, I would still have thought that Grauman's Chinese was the largest and most beautiful.

The curtain went up, and the stage show began. The Rockettes' precision dancing was almost unbelievable. The beauty of the girls, their costumes, and their famous high kicks seemed unsurpassed. I had never seen anything like them. They had to love what they were doing. I had heard that in addition to the six shows a day, they constantly rehearsed for the future show. It had to be hard work, and I wondered if they ever saw daylight. I admired them greatly since I knew a little of what it took to get there.

While I had the chance, I rode the subway to see Macy's, advertised as the world's largest department store. I wandered in the shoe department trying to find something my size when a gentleman approached. "I notice you have small feet and am wondering if you're a size 4-B?"

"Yes," I told him, "I am. Why?"

"Do you know that 4-Bs are sample sizes?"

"Yes, I do," I said. "In Hollywood I used to buy sample shoes at the Cinderella Slipper Shop. It was wonderful knowing that every shoe in the store would fit me."

He smiled and asked, "How would you like to model shoes for buyers looking for various styles to sell in their stores?" That sounded good, so for awhile, I became a shoe model.

*Accidentally Yours*, a fast-moving comedy, had booked a run at the Montclair Theater in New Jersey. This stage production starred Grant Mitchell, who had been in many movies, including *Leave Her to Heaven* and *Laura*. The cast also included Paula Trueman, Lynn Carter, and Craig Stevens. The producer had been looking for an actress to play the part of a genie. I showed up at the interview with several other girls. One by one, we read some lines, and I ended up with the part, thrilled for the opportunity to wear a beautiful costume and look glamorous, especially after being cast as Fanny Frobisher in *Heaven on Earth* two months earlier.

After going through the usual rehearsals, we opened. The theater filled with Broadway first-nighters who made the trip especially to see this show. During this three-act play, theatergoers howled with laughter. Everyone seemed to be having a great time, including me.

The next day, when the reviews hit the streets, the *New York Sun* gave us an excellent review, saying, in part, "Caren Marsh, as the genie who comes to the professor's rescue, is a delightful eyeful."

*The New York Journal-American's* review was just as enthusiastic: "*Accidentally Yours* is a promising farce tinged with fantasy." In the same column was, "Caren Marsh, as the genie, is indeed, an eyeful."

With little sister Dorothy in 1925

Caren, the six-year-old ballerina

My first trip to the desert. This is the road to Palm Springs Village,
1924 (courtesy P.S. Historical Society)

Bathhouse with mineral springs in Palm Springs,
1920s. (courtesy P.S. Historical Society)

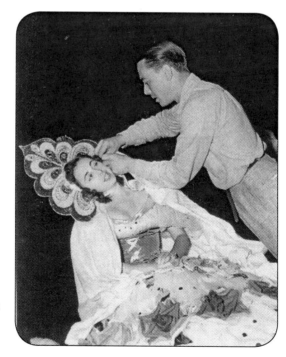

Right out of Hollywood
High school and into my
first dance job, in MGM's
*Rosalie* in 1937. I'm having
my headdress adjusted
between takes. Eleanor
Powell starred in this lavish
Musical

Lunching with Judy Garland and her teacher in the MGM commissary
during the making of *The Wizard of Oz*. I was Judy's stand -in.

*That Night in Rio* starred Alice Faye and Don Ameche.
I'm fourth dancing girl from the right. 1941

*My Best Gal*, starring Jane Withers and Jimmy Lydon, 1944.
I am dancing on the counter.

*Best Foot Forward*, 1943. I'm second from the left in the first row.

*Hit Parade of 1943.* I am dancing with my partner on the third drum from left.

The prom in *Best Foot Forward*, MGM, 1943

*Nobody' Darling*, 1943. I'm third from left in dance line.

*Secrets of a Sorority Girl*, 1946. I am second from left.

Dance sequence from *Hands Across the Border*, 1943.
I'm the second cowgirl from the right.

Cutting my birthday cake in a scene from *The Navajo Kid*, 1945.

With Bob Steele and his sidekick, Syd Saylor.

Bob Steele's leading lady
in *The Navajo Kid*, 1945.

Publicity Picture from
*Hit Parade of 1943*.

With my dance partner
in *Hit Parade of 1943*,
Republic Pictures. This
starred Susan Hayward
and was also known as
*Change of Heart*.

*The Navajo Kid* lobby card, 1945.

*Secrets of a Sorority Girl* lobby
card, 1946

With Roy Rogers in *Hands
Across the Border*, 1943

*My Best Gal* lobby card, 1944.

*Carew's Sister*

Donna Reed, Mickey Rooney, Dorothy Morris, and
Fay Bainter in *The Human Comedy*, 1943.

*Hands Across the Border* lobby card, 1943.

Ella Raines, Joan Blondell, Heather Angel, Dorothy Morris, Margaret
Sullavan, Frances Gifford, Diana Lewis, Ann Sothern, and Marsha
Hunt in *Cry Havoc*, MGM, 1943.

4-H girl on a farm.
Publicity for the movie
*Wild Harvest*, 1947.

More publicity for
*Wild Harvest*.

Standing on wing of a plane after winning the "Miss Skylady of 1947" contest.

Publicity portrait for "Miss Skylady of 1947."

Refueling the plane.

This is a copy of one of the leaflets
that appeared in a Los Angeles
newspaper.

Publicity by the cockpit with
headphones and microphone.

With Robert Preston, Dick Erdman, Allen
Jenkins, Lloyd Nolan, and Alan Ladd in a scene
from *Wild Harvest*. Dick Erdman, who played my
husband, will forever be remembered for his
numerous films, including *Stalag 17*.

As a 4-H girl with Alan Ladd, who starred in
Paramount's *Wild Harvest*, 1947.

On the set with Kirk Douglas. He is pouring me a glass of chocolate milk.

On the set of *I Walk Alone* with Kirk Douglas, 1947.

At Paramount, on the set of *I Walk Alone* with Kirk Douglas, 1947.

With Errol Flynn in *Adventures of Don Juan*, Warner Bros.

With Alan Hale on the set of
*Adventures of Don Juan.*

With James Stewart on the Paramount lot where
he was working on his latest film.

Chatting with Orson Welles
on the set of *Macbeth*, 1947.

Red Skelton takes
my picture for publicity.

With Bing Crosby on the set of *Welcome Stranger*.

One of my dance costumes.

During rehearsals with the star of the Broadway musical,
Peter Lind Hayes. I'm in the center.

On the stage with Jackie
Cooper in *Sleep It Off*,
1948.

Publicity photo by a Beverly Hills
swimming pool.

On the stage in *Accidentally Yours*, 1948.

I received this photo from the newsmen at Acme
News Service. I was "Tops" on their tree.

Playing "The Genie" in the stage production of *Accidentally Yours*, 1948, in Montclair, New Jersey.

# Chapter Thirteen

The play finished its two-week run and several months later Paul Winchell, the ventriloquist, interviewed and hired me for his television show. The sketches we did together with his wooden dummy, Jerry Mahoney, was another new experience for me. After working with Paul, he told me he was going to appear on stage at the Capitol Theater the following month. He asked if I would like to do a sketch with him. A chance to appear at the Capitol on Broadway? Of course. He would be doing his act as part of the stage show before the movie.

It was July 1949, and since I had a month before the job started, I wanted to go home to visit my parents and family. It had been a long time, and I missed them. Before leaving, Paul handed me a contract with starting salary and a date he wanted me back.

"We'll only need a couple of rehearsals," he said.

I was glad to have the contract in my hot little hands. If my parents tried to talk me into staying in Hollywood, I would show them the contract that had to be honored. I phoned home and told them, "I'll fly out of here on the fifteenth and have three weeks with you before I have to be back for rehearsals."

We were all excited about seeing each other again—it had been over a year. Then they asked if I could leave a few days earlier and attend a cousin's wedding on the twelfth. It was short notice, but I told them I'd try to get a flight out. I tried, but there wasn't a seat available that would get me there in time. I wouldn't make the wedding, but I would see them on the fifteenth, as scheduled.

The next evening at a friend's home, I told them of my disappointment. One of the guests mentioned that she knew a pilot who flew for Standard Air Service, an unscheduled airline, and she might be able to get me a flight the next day.

After making a phone call, she returned all smiles. "You're set for tomorrow evening on a seven-thirty flight out of La Guardia. The plane will arrive at eight the next morning at Lockheed Air Terminal in Burbank, California. You'll be there the morning of the wedding."

What luck. I phoned home with the good news, attended to last-minute plans, then at seven o'clock on the eleventh, I was at La Guardia ready to leave. I wore my favorite navy blue, silk shantung sheath and navy high heel pumps, wanting to look my best when I stepped off the plane. I carried my fur stole and scrapbook. My seat assignment was third seat from the rear of the plane, by a window. Next to me, on the aisle, a young woman mentioned that her husband was a pilot.

At seven-thirty, we taxied out in the twin-engine plane, and I saw my friends wave goodbye. I waved back, looking forward to a pleasant flight to my hometown. The martini I had with friends before leaving made me sleepy so I leaned back and dozed off.

I woke up when we landed somewhere to gas up. I tried to go back to sleep. When I awoke later, it was getting light, and I knew we should be arriving in Burbank. Flying coast-to-coast had been a twelve-hour flight. It was tiresome, but I was almost there. We were on our final approach to Burbank airport. My seat belt was fastened. My mother would be waiting for me.

Suddenly, a roaring, crashing impact and the sound of screech-ing metal felt like the belly of the plane bumped and dragged on the ground. The plane shook violently—people screamed. My body lurched from side to side in my seat. My window and the side of the plane had caved in against me.

"We've crashed, but this can't be happening to me," shot through my mind. "This must be a nightmare. This couldn't be real,"

Then—all was deadly quiet. I heard crackling sounds. Flames shot up ahead; I sat there in a daze. I couldn't move. I became aware that the pilot's wife sitting next to me was unbuckling my seat belt and saying, "We've got to get out of here fast." I saw bloody cuts on her face and instinctively put my hands to mine to see if I was bleeding too; I wasn't. She pulled me up from my collapsed seat and grabbing me by the arm, dragged me along with her toward the open exit door. Before we could reach it, we were in the belly of the plane that had been torn apart. While flames were crackling around us, she dragged me out of the plane and into the brush. Numbed, I stood there and looked around to get my bearings.

"My God," I cried out.

I was on a mountainside next to a burning airplane. Someone yelled, "Get away from that plane before it explodes!"

That jolted me. I desperately scrambled down the side of the moun-tain following the pilot's wife. Brush and brambles tore my dress to shreds. My nightmare increased every second. I saw some bodies ly-ing in the brush. My left foot flopped around like a rag doll. When I glanced down it didn't look like a foot, it resembled raw hamburger with white noodles sticking up. A toe was split wide open to the bone. How could my foot look so ghastly and not cause pain? And why didn't I faint at the sight of it?

I continued to crawl until I reached a dirt road below. A few passengers lay there on the ground. I felt so weary and couldn't seem to get enough air in my lungs. I gasped for breath and collapsed exhausted. I had no sense of time—no feeling.

White-robed figures walked slowly around me in an ethereal scene. Who were they? Angels? Had I died?

A man carrying a little black satchel approached me. "Is there anything I can do to help you?"

"Please notify my mother, she's waiting at the airport for me. Tell her I'm all right."

He took her name and promised to get word to her when he found out where I would be taken. I glanced up the mountainside at the smoldering, twisted pieces of what had once been an airplane

I wondered how I had ever gotten out alive. It seemed like ages before the ambulances arrived. I expected blood to be pouring out of my bloody foot by now. There was none. And still no pain.

They carried me down the mountain on a stretcher and held my shredded dress together around me. The wail of the siren was a blessed sound to me as we raced to Van Nuys Receiving Hospital.

The attendant who rode with me sadly said, "They'll probably have to take your foot off. There's nothing much left of it."

I couldn't comprehend his words—what was he saying? My poor foot. How would I walk? How could I dance?

Inside the hospital they put my stretcher alongside others in the hallway. My dress was hanging off me in shreds. I looked at my crushed left foot again and burst into sobs. They can't cut my foot off—they can't—they can't!

Suddenly I heard my parents' voices. I looked up and there they were bending over me with tears of relief streaming down their faces.

That man had kept his promise and notified my mother. The airport had paged her over the loudspeaker and she was told to go to the phone. Then she called Daddy at work. They rushed me immediately to Cedars of Lebanon Hospital in a private ambulance where one of the best surgeons in town waited for me.

Upon my arrival, he treated what was left of my foot, sewed up the split toe, and put my foot in a cast up to my shin. The doctor said it was a miracle that parts of my body hadn't been slashed on impact. I was badly bruised and all the damage had been done to my left foot.

I asked the surgeon, "How come there's been no pain?"

"Because," he said, "your nerves and tendons were severed and no pain was reaching your brain."

"The white noodles I saw?"

"Yes, your tendons. You'll start feeling pain now, but we'll take care of that. You'll be comfortable."

Having been given Demerol, I went to sleep with my world crashing around me in my head. But I knew I would be all right. I just had to be. I had a lot of living to do. I thanked God that I was alive and in one piece.

When I woke up, a nurse had brought in a newspaper reporter. Later, a cameraman ran film on me that would appear in theater newsreels. I knew I looked a mess, but that wasn't important to me. The twenty-five-dollar cost for a private room concerned me, a lot of money for my parents to spend.

I remembered those white-robed figures I had seen on the mountain after the accident. I asked about them—nobody seemed to know.

Beautiful flowers started arriving, and my large room soon overflowed with them. I asked the nurse to please take some of them to the children's ward. "Just save the cards," I told her, "so I'll know who sent them."

Telegrams poured in from families of those who hadn't survived the crash. They all asked the same questions: Did you know my sister? Did you talk to my brother during the flight?

Later, get-well cards arrived from people all over the country that I'd never met: I realized how wonderful and compassionate people could be.

When I asked about the accident, and what happened, I was told that apparently the pilot had been making his approach to the airport too low over the mountains. The plane's right wing hit a large boulder and was ripped off. The fuselage tore ahead into the heavy brush and burst into flames near Chatsworth, California. Chatsworth? How ironic. That was where I had been on location with Bob Steele two years earlier. If anyone had pointed to those mountains then, and told me, "Caren, two years from now you will be crawling out of a burning plane up there," I'd have called them crazy.

When the papers came out with stories and photos of the crash, I learned who those white-robed figures were at the scene. One article read: "The bearded and barefoot men in white robes were from a monastery in Box Canyon. They had rushed to the mountain to help victims."

Another article reported that firefighters from Ventura County Fire Department were among those responding to the crash. I also read that the aircraft had been a former military, twin-engine, C-46 cargo plane, licensed and converted for passenger travel. And I was surprised to read that we had scrambled down the mountain 500 yards to reach the fire road.

In one of the papers, I appeared in a picture in my hospital bed, looking terrible, and underneath were the words, Acme Photo. A few years earlier, I had received a photograph from the reporters at Acme News Service around Christmas. In the photo was a picture of a Christmas tree on a table in their newsroom. Perched on top of their tree was a cutout of me in a two-piece swimsuit. My picture had been sent out to the wire services by one of the studio publicity departments months before. On the photo someone had written, "Caren, you're tops on our tree. Acme."

The surgeon, who had saved my foot, came in to see me every day. He told me, "It will be all right. You'll be able to walk on it again, Caren, but I'm sorry to have to tell you that you won't be able to dance again or wear high heels. Your foot was badly crushed."

Not dance again? No high heels? I refused to let those thoughts enter my mind. Since I'd be in the hospital until the end of the month, I promised myself to take all that time to picture myself in high heels and dancing again. I knew I would.

While recovering, I received a call from ventriloquist Paul Winchell in New York, asking how I was and would I still be able to appear with him on August 15 at the Capitol Theater.

My nurse told him that'd be impossible. I'd brought my contract as my excuse to return to New York even against the wishes of my parents. Now the contract had probably burned up in the plane, along with my purse, scrapbook, and suitcase. So much for planning ahead.

The phone rang again and my second call from New York. "Hello Caren, it's Bill."

Bill Doll, my dear friend who was a press agent in New York, caused me to smile.

"Your picture has been on the front pages saying you survived an awful crash," he said. "I'm coming to see you."

"Bill, I want to see you too, but I'm scared to have you fly."

"I'll come by train, honey. So don't worry."

Three days on the train to get here, and three days to return. "How long can you stay?"

"Two days. I didn't realize how much you meant to me until now. I love you. See you in a few days."

We hung up, and I smiled as I remembered the first time we met while I was in *Heaven on Earth*. He was the show's press agent. How strange—his face had flashed across my mind while I waited for an ambulance on that mountainside. Now he would be coming to see me.

Time dragged on, and I took Demerol to kill the pain. It made me feel dreamy, as if I was floating. I felt better when the nurse surprised me one day with some publicity pictures from my scrapbook. Some people had gone up on the mountain to observe the crash sight and found them strewn all over the mountainside. They thought I'd like to have them so they brought them to the hospital. It was so thoughtful, and I would have liked to have thanked them. Many of the photos and clippings had burned around the edges, others had been torn, but I was happy to have them.

My parents visited every day. During one of their visits I told them, "I think I know what it would be like to die. I realize even if my body hadn't survived the crash, I would have survived. I'd still be me." It's strange how near-devastating experiences in our lives can sometimes bring about thoughts, or insights, like that.

Three days had gone by when the door of my room opened, and Bill peeked around the corner. I didn't know I'd be so happy to see him. Mother and Daddy were there and met Bill. I believe they sensed why he had come.

Bill spent the afternoon with me and asked, "Honey, what's your favorite restaurant?"

"Don the Beachcomber in Hollywood. Why?"

"Just wondered," he said. "When you're out of the hospital, we'll go there."

"Oh, Bill, I'd like that very much."

Early that evening the door opened. Instead of the nurse bringing in my dinner, it was a smiling Bill and a waiter from Don the Beachcomber. The waiter had a huge tray covered with dishes, and two rum navy grogs.

"I can't believe this," I said. My salivary glands worked overtime as I lifted the cover of each dish and inhaled the heavenly aroma. My favorites: baby spareribs, chicken livers and chestnuts wrapped in bacon, and almond duck with all the extras. It had been over a year since I had tasted such delicious food. What a wonderful surprise.

"I hope you don't get into trouble bringing all this food in here. They must have rules about that," I told him, as I reached for the navy grog.

"I got an okay from the hospital before I ordered, honey. I hope it makes you happy."

"Bill, thank you, thank you. It was so sweet of you to do this."

The nurse entered on cue and saw the navy grog. "Sorry, Caren," she said. "You can't drink that. You're on medication, and they don't mix."

"Could I just stick my tongue in the glass? A teeny taste, maybe?"

"A teeny taste," she said.

I stuck my tongue in the glass, and then handed the drink to Bill, "Looks like you're going to have to finish this for me."

I began to examine my true feelings toward this thoughtful, caring man, thinking, it wouldn't be hard to fall in love with him.

Bill's two days with me passed quickly, and it was time for him to leave. He said, "I'll be back to see you next month—by train again—so don't worry. You should be home by then. It's been wonderful seeing you." Before he left, he told me, "You know, when that picture of you and that story appeared in the papers, it made me so sick I threw up. It made me question why I reacted like that. Now I know."

I think we both knew.

The end of the month arrived, and the surgeon removed the cast and put another small, removable one on my foot. The doctor said, "You have to soak your foot several times a day. The flesh will eventually fill in. When it's healed, your foot will be badly gnarled, but plastic surgery will take care of that." He handed me a pair of crutches. "You'll be using these for another month, then you can start taking steps without them." I didn't want to wait that long. I continued to picture my foot healing—soon.

By the middle of summer, I was home again, and Bill made his second trip to see me. When he arrived, I was soaking my foot as the doctor ordered. My wounds healed slowly, but when Bill saw my foot, I thought he was going to throw up.

"It does look terrible," he said. "How long do the doctors say it will be until it looks like a foot again?"

I shook my head. Neither of us could even guess.

"You poor darling," he said, studying my foot. "You've been through a helluva lot."

When time came for him to leave, he said, "I'll be back next month to see you. I love you."

Get-well letters that arrived at the hospital were forwarded on to me. Bing Crosby sent one—very thoughtful—I had only worked one day with him.

I continued to soak my foot. The flesh began to fill in somewhat. A friend of Mother's visited me one day. I told her that even when it healed, I'd still have to have plastic surgery.

"No, you won't, Caren," she said rather emphatically. "That foot of yours will be perfect, and it's not going to take as long a time as you were told. You'll see."

What does she know? She's not a doctor.

Mother's friend continued to visit me every week. After one visit, I called, "Mother, come in here and look at my foot. Is it just my imagination, or has more flesh filled in since your friend's visit?"

She stood over me and, after carefully studying my foot, said, "No, Babe, it's not your imagination, I see it too. It has actually grown flesh very quickly."

"How do you figure that?"

"Well, honey, my friend is a Christian Science Practitioner. She wanted to visit you and see if she could help. I don't really know what she does, or what a 'practitioner' really is, but I will say, your foot didn't look this good before she started seeing you."

Amazing. Whatever she did, I was grateful for it.

Bill called with good news. He'd been hired to publicize a movie in Hollywood. This time he would be able to stay for three weeks. He still sent me a special delivery letter every day. They arrived at eleven o'clock every night, and when the postman rang our doorbell, he didn't have to ring twice.

Every day I noticed my foot looked better and better. Like a miracle, it fascinated me the way the flesh was filling in. I wanted to see my foot healed by the time Bill arrived so we could go to Don the Beachcombers as he promised. I walked well with the crutches by then, and looked forward to the day when I could throw them aside and walk on my own. The pain continued, and I still took Demerol.

One time I called out—"Mother, I need some Demerol."

"Is the pain still bad?" she asked.

"No, but the Demerol will help."

"Babe, you're not going to have any more. It can be habit forming."

I pleaded with her. "Just this one more time, please."

"No," she said. "You can start taking those pills the doctor said to give to you."

"I don't want those. I want the Demerol. Please, please."

"No, Babe." She said emphatically. Was I really becoming dependent on it? I loved that floating feeling. But I couldn't go on floating—I wanted to dance. And I couldn't dance if I got hooked on that drug. I was determined to dance again and realized what I had to do.

"All right," I said, reluctantly, "give me the other pills."

Like a baby learning to walk, best describes my first steps without the crutches. When Bill arrived for his three-week stay, I still used the crutches but went everywhere with him. We lunched with columnists and dined with important business people.

The night at Don the Beachcombers, I looked forward to the food and navy grog. The tropical island atmosphere made me happy. We ordered drinks and appetizers. Suddenly I began to feel strange, different somehow, as if the ceiling was coming slowly down on my head and the walls were gradually closing in on me.

I thought, Oh God, I'm going to be crushed. "Bill," I said, in a near panic, "I have to leave this minute. Everything is closing in on me. I'm going to be crushed!"

"Honey, our drinks and your favorite appetizers are coming. Don't you want them?"

I sobbed. "I've got to get out of here, or I'll be crushed."

I grabbed my crutches, lifted myself out of the seat and, with Bill's help, headed for the door. He hailed a cab, and we rode back to the house—his comforting arm around me.

"Honey, you're shaking," he said.

I tried to imagine what had happened to me. My head was in a turmoil. If I had stayed, would I really have been crushed? How often would this unexpected terror come back to haunt me?

Months had passed. My foot felt more alive and stronger. The flesh had filled in, but my legs remained weak from lack of exercise. I decided to see my ballet teacher, Mr. Kosloff, for exercises that would strengthen my dancing muscles. I knew I'd never fit into toe shoes again, or even wear tap shoes. But I knew I must somehow dance again.

Bill's visits continued, and our feelings for each other grew. We both sensed a solid love that bound us together. He had certainly shown his devotion and made many sacrifices so he could be with me during those rough times. Our love had progressed to the point that we began to talk marriage.

One evening, when Bill joined us for dinner, Mother had made some of her delicious chicken soup. As I put my spoon in the bowl, white noodles floated to the top. I burst into sobs and shook violently. I couldn't look at those noodles. What was happening to me? I saw a burning airplane, people screaming, my foot torn and bloody as I waited for help. Visions—horrible visions—returned to haunt me. I excused myself and hobbled into the other room. I couldn't stop shaking and sobbing. Would this continue the rest of my life? My parents and Bill, while upset and concerned, seemed to understand more than I did why I reacted that way.

# Chapter Fourteen

Bill had to return to his business in New York, but he didn't want to go back without me. By that time, we had decided to get married. His New York responsibilities made our decision easy. We drove to Las Vegas, and as the minister in the little chapel said the words:

"Do you take this man to be your lawfully wedded husband?"

"I do." Bill slipped the ring on my finger.

"I now pronounce you man and wife. You may kiss the bride."

And that was it. I was Mrs. Bill Doll. My parents attended, but my sister and her husband couldn't make it. With two kids to look after, it just wasn't possible.

Three days later we arrived in New York and rented an apartment on the West Side of Manhattan, four blocks from Central Park. Life with Bill was wonderful, and I knew I had made the right choice. We enjoyed being together. I would have a martini waiting for him when he came home from work, and we dined by candlelight.

Bill's office was on the second floor of the Algonquin Hotel on West 44th Street. We ate lunch in the dining room one day when I asked him, "What about this famous Algonquin Round Table I've heard so much about?"

Bill stopped eating for a moment and said, "The Round Table

was a group made up of newspaper people, drama and movie critics, playwrights, authors, columnists and novelists."

"How did all this come about? Who were some of these people?"

"Did you ever hear of Alexander Woollcott?" he asked. "He inspired *The Man Who Came to Dinner*. You might not have seen the play, but you must have seen the movie starring Monty Woolley."

"Yes, I've heard of Woollcott, and I saw the movie."

"Well, Woollcott founded the group in the '20s. He had a large, round table put into the center of the dining room where the group lunched every day. The dining room was always filled with customers who came to see these famous people, and perhaps, overhear some of the brilliant conversations they had about the theatre."

I looked around the room and imagined them all there as we lunched. Yes, I would have liked to have seen them. A bit of show business history in the making.

After lunch, Bill had to make a phone call. He led me across the lobby, and we headed for his office. As we stepped in the elevator, he pointed to a stack of papers lying on the floor behind the elevator operator's feet, placed there for the convenience of the guests.

"That's where I first saw the news of your plane crash, honey. I was on my way up to the office, and there were the headlines and your picture, staring up at me. I was shocked. It made me sick to think of you in that mess, not knowing how badly you were injured."

It had been over a year, but seemed like a lifetime. I was so thankful to be there with Bill, and in one piece.

Like most men involved in the newspaper business, Bill drank quite a bit, a dubious reputation they all shared. I tried not to be too concerned about it. After all, I enjoyed my martini before dinner, same as Bill. I remembered my first drink of Rum and Coke made me a little wobbly, but I'm a small person. I'd heard that, the larger a person is, the better they are able to handle alcohol. Bill was six feet tall, but strangely, one drink appeared to affect him. Was I missing something?

When Bill publicized a show, the producer or director welcomed me to sit in the theater during rehearsal. I felt fortunate to watch those fabulous artists on the stage. Some eventually went to Hollywood and became major stars.

Bill told me one evening that we would be traveling to different towns with the show *Peter Pan*. I was thrilled. It would be nice traveling with a show again. "How's that for an unexpected honeymoon?" he said.

The show starred Jean Arthur and Boris Karloff. Jean Arthur had been in many movies, including those I had seen: Mr. *Deeds Goes to Town, You Can't Take it With You* and *The Devil and Miss Jones*. She had that husky voice that, to me, was always so appealing. She had just won critical acclaim for her performance in *Peter Pan* on Broadway. Now they were taking it on the road.

We left on the train five days ahead of the others. I'd only toured once before, and I was one of the actors, so traveling ahead was all new to me.

I asked, "Why do we travel to all these cities ahead of the cast? Won't we miss the opening nights?"

"The press agent does the advance publicity," he explained. "So we have to travel ahead of the show. I'll be spending a lot of time with the newspaper guys and with the theater owners. That means lunches and dinners with them as well."

I wasn't sure, before Bill's explanation, just what it was a press agent did for a road show—how important a job it was.

"By the time the show arrives," he said, "everyone in town will know about it. And yes, we will be there for the opening night, and a few days after. Then we'll move on to the next town while the play is here for its run."

When we arrived, we took a cab to a hotel where reservations had been made for us. "It'll work this way in every town," Bill said.

I enjoyed every minute of it, the hotels, the room service, dining with the newspaper people, opening nights, and the parties afterward.

During the day, Bill had appointments but always invited me to join him for his business lunches, and sometimes I did. Other times I window-shopped, took in a movie, or simply walked around sightseeing. We were always together in the evenings, even if only for a dinner meeting.

One morning Jean Arthur called Bill in our hotel room and told him she couldn't make an interview with a reporter that afternoon because of a miserable cold—she just didn't feel up to it.

I told Bill, "I don't see how she could possibly fly back and forth tonight on those wires, sneezing and blowing her nose. It's tough enough having to do that act when you feel good."

Bill went to see her. When he returned, he smiled. "Can you beat that?" he said. "She was sitting up in bed eating a bowl of caviar. She said that was the only thing that cures her colds. How's that for a remedy?"

"Some expensive cure," I said.

Expensive or not, there was Peter Pan flying high above the stage that night, and without a runny nose. The show must go on!

The tour finally ended, and we returned to New York. Bill called from the office one afternoon around two o'clock. He sounded drunk. Drunk at two in the afternoon? Did I say something that morning to upset him so much he would get drunk? Was I making him unhappy? I didn't know what to do except wait for him to come home and ask him. I expected him around six that evening, but no Bill. At eight o'clock, I called his office. No answer. At nine, I really worried, for fear he'd been in an accident. But no one had phoned with any bad news. By ten o'clock I started to panic, when I heard his key in the lock. He opened the door, staggered in, gave me a silly grin, then headed for the bedroom. He flopped on the bed and fell sound asleep, and snored. I couldn't believe this was happening. Tears soon streamed down my cheeks.

His snoring kept me up all night, but I doubted I could have slept even if it were quiet; there was so much on my mind. In the morning, Bill pulled himself out of bed to make it to the office at his usual hour. It amazed me he could even move. I waited for an explanation.

All I heard was, "I'm sorry. It won't happen again. I love you."

But it did happen again—and again.

One of the big hotels on the Las Vegas strip wanted some publicity in New York and hired Bill. We arrived at the El Rancho, and they assigned us a bungalow instead of one of their standard rooms. I looked forward to an enjoyable three months and spent my afternoons by the pool while Bill worked.

In the evenings we dressed for the dinner shows. I was amazed that we could sit at a table and watch the late shows for as little as a piece of pie and a cup of coffee with no cover, no minimum, and a spectacular show. During our three months in Las Vegas, we saw every show at every hotel with a variety of entertainment. We made many friends while there, and Bill made some strong business contacts and new clients.

Every night after the late show, we would return to our bungalow, and Bill would type a report about the hotel amenities, including accommodations, entertainment, celebrity guests, and other items of interest that would be good publicity and draw new customers from New York.

By four in the morning Bill had finished, and we would go to the dining room for the Chuck Wagon Breakfast Buffet. On the way, he dropped his report to the New York papers in the lobby mail slot.

It wasn't unusual to see the same people still gambling at the tables that we had seen the night before. Some were so-called, "High Rollers." They spent a lot of money and received V.I.P. treatment from the hotel.

My gambling was usually allotted to a few nickels in the slot machines after dinner. I think the most I ever won was three dollars. After a hearty breakfast, we would go to bed and sleep until noon, and then we'd start the day all over again. At the end of our three months, I had had a wonderful time, mostly because Bill hadn't had even one drink.

One of Bill's next publicity jobs was with a studio in Hollywood. We took the train back for our first visit since I had moved to New York. While in Hollywood, I decided to show my now-healed foot to the surgeon who had saved it two years earlier. He greeted me with a hug, and told me, "Caren, you're a lucky girl to have survived such a terrible crash. And I see you're walking in high-heeled boots." He asked how long we would be in town, and the possibility of doing some plastic surgery on my instep to smooth it out.

I surprised him by pulling off my boot and sock. "Look at my foot," I said.

I could see by his expression that he was amazed at the appearance of my instep. The last time he had seen it there was simply red, raw flesh. It was now smooth with only a faint, white scar.

"Well, what do you think?" I asked him.

"Caren," he said. "I've been a surgeon for many years and have never seen anything heal as fast as your foot and not need plastic surgery afterwards. It's remarkable." I told him about the Christian Science Practitioner who I thought had a lot to do with the healing. "I don't know anything about Christian Science, but this lady visited me every week, and after every visit, more flesh had filled in. And it wasn't my imagination, Mother saw it too."

After examining my foot closely, the doctor said, "Caren, I have to tell you that when I have a patient with a condition where nothing more can be done, I have always suggested a Christian Science Practitioner. No, you certainly don't need any plastic surgery now."

I had heard about doctors being called in on cases where Christian Science had failed. Now here was a new twist—a doctor suggesting a practitioner as a last resort. Well, whatever works? I was just grateful it worked for me. I felt great and looked forward to two wonderful weeks in California.

I was lying around the pool one day at my sister Dorothy's home in North Hollywood, when she asked, "Don't you miss dancing? It's been so long."

"Of course I do," I told her. "Don't you miss your acting?"

"Absolutely not," she said. "This is the best role I've ever had. I love being a full-time mother to our two wonderful sons."

"Well," I said, "I'd really love to dance again, but I can't wear dance shoes."

"Sis, I have a friend who taught Hawaiian dancing in Hawaii. She lives a few blocks from here and takes care of the Ruth St. Denis Dance Studio. I could arrange for her to give you private lessons right here by the pool before you have to leave for New York."

The thought intrigued me. Hawaiian dancing—so beautiful. Always loved the music and I remembered Harry Owens, his Royal Hawaiians, and his three Hawaiian dancers, at the Beverly Wilshire Hotel. "Yes, please call her," I said.

She returned moments later. "If you and Bill don't have plans, she can be here tomorrow morning."

"We have no plans, so let's do it as soon as possible."

Dancing had been my life, and the thought of dancing again brought back some beautiful memories, and a personal resolve to continue dancing as long as I could. Right on schedule my teacher, Dorothy Tifal, arrived. She showed me how to move my feet—my bare feet—no shoes required. She explained other movements and their meanings. "The swaying of the hips, for example, is taken from the swaying of the palm trees."

I practiced until I learned to sway smoothly. Then she taught me some of the hand movements that tell a story to the lyrics of the music. It was a graceful dance, and I was in heaven. I took more lessons, and she taught me three dances, including the hip-shaking Tahitian dance. I wanted to learn as much as possible before we had to leave.

One day Bill conducted business with some writers and newspaper columnists. We had planned to meet at five o'clock in our hotel room before having dinner at my parents' home. At five I entered the room, and there was Bill, intoxicated. I was angry and disappointed. It seemed that whether it was New York, California, or wherever, when he was with those newspaper people that's what happened.

I hated the thought that my parents would see him like that. Why did he get drunk? Did I upset him in some way? Was it the dancing lessons, taking up time we should have spent together? Those thoughts churned through my mind as I looked into his bleary eyes. I could hardly hold back the tears.

We arrived for dinner. Bill wasn't a falling down kind of drunk—but he was unsteady on his feet with that silly, stupid grin on his face. I could tell that my parents were upset to see him that way, but they didn't mention his condition. Damn it, Bill, how could you humiliate yourself and me in front of my parents?

Before we were married, I knew Bill drank. Sometimes I saw him drunk. But I attributed it to unhappiness. I thought if I could make him happy, he wouldn't feel the need to get drunk. He often said he'd never been happier than when he was with me.

Then why did he drink? What did I do wrong?

He always apologized the next morning, saying, "It won't happen again."

But it did.

I loved Bill and was so happy when he was his sober self. I thought back about our life together, and I liked it. We'd had fun while Bill conducted business, the out-of-town tryouts we attended in New Haven, Boston and Philadelphia, and the train rides, the opening nights sitting around Sardi's waiting for the reviews that were read aloud to all those present, the cheers after the good reviews, the somber faces after the poor ones. I had enjoyed all that. While no longer in show business myself, I remained a part of it. Bill's drinking made it a bittersweet combination.

The following morning Mother asked the question I had dreaded: "Does Bill do this frequently?"

I knew I couldn't fool her.

"Yes, I'm afraid so. I love him, and I don't know what to do."

"Babe," she said, "our neighbor told me that she used to get drunk all the time. She's been going to AA and hasn't had a drink in years. Why don't you ask her about it? Maybe she can help."

At the time, the only AA I knew was American Airlines.

When I went over to see this lady, she said she'd been sober for ten years. She said, "I'm attending a meeting this afternoon. Would you like to go with me?"

"Yes, I would," I told her and asked if I could bring a friend whose husband had a drinking problem.

When I called my friend, she wanted very much to go with us, saying, "Maybe we'll both find out why our husbands drink."

At the meeting in Hollywood, we saw a cross-section of people. Some looked neat and well dressed; others a bit shabby around the edges. A man stood up, gave his first name, and said, "I'm an alcoholic."

What an eye opener for me. This nice-looking man was an alcoholic? He talked of his drinking experience and how he finally came to Alcoholics Anonymous. "I've been sober now for five years," he told the group.

One-by-one, others stood up, stated their first names and added, "I'm an alcoholic."

One gentleman told us, "If it was raining, it was an excuse to get drunk. If the sun was shining, just another excuse to drink. To an alcoholic, anything is an excuse to hit the bottle. Then after that first drink, it's all downhill."

Another man said, "I was one of those drunks you see lying in a doorway with a bottle in a paper bag. It doesn't happen overnight. For some of us we first lost our jobs, then our families. And that's where you end up if you don't get wise and seek help. It's either AA, or the graveyard."

Still another man said, "We're not just heavy drinkers—someone who can stop when we want to—we're alcoholics, and we can't stop, even if we want to. I'm thankful for AA. I've been sober for nine years."

After listening to these people, I felt a tremendous sense of relief. I realized I wasn't the cause of Bill's drinking. He was an alcoholic! All the torment I had been going through, wondering what I had been doing wrong, had nothing to do with me. I didn't have to blame myself anymore.

It seemed clear then as I turned to my friend and said, "How about that, now we know why our husbands get drunk, even when they don't intend to. They're alcoholics." The solution appeared simple. Get them both to these AA meetings, and they won't drink again. I could see everything coming up roses.

She surprised me when she said, "Everything I've heard here this afternoon sounds familiar. I realize that both my husband and I are alcoholics. I'm going to start coming to these meetings, and I hope he comes with me."

I hadn't expected that revelation. My beautiful little friend—an alcoholic.

I learned the Serenity Prayer that afternoon:

> God grant me the serenity
> To accept the things I cannot change
> Courage to change the things I can, and the
> Wisdom to know the difference.

I didn't realize then that I would be using it on many occasions throughout the rest of my life.

# Chapter Fifteen

Bill and I had planned a cruise to the Virgin Islands and Haiti after we returned to New York. I figured we would both go to AA meetings following the trip. If he got drunk on the cruise, at least I would know it wasn't my fault. That thought brought me some relief.

It had been a good vacation. Bill returned to his old self, sober and lots of fun. After the cruise, we attended the opening night of a Broadway show, Leonard Sillman's *New Faces of 1952*, and a party afterwards. Several of those faces, went on to big careers: Eartha Kitt, Paul Lynde, Carol Lawrence, Robert Clary, and Alice Ghostley, among them.

At the party, I couldn't help but notice a stunning redhead. I recognized her as a dancer at MGM when I worked there. "Hi, Judi, remember me? MGM?"

She jumped up, "Caren, how wonderful to see you again. What are you doing in New York?"

"The press agent is my husband. I live here now. What about you?"

"I'm married and live here too," she said. "What do you do now to keep busy? Could we have lunch and talk about our dancing days?"

I asked if she was free on Wednesday, but she declined. "I give a lot of my time to my church work, so Wednesday is out. How about another day?"

Church work? I never asked people what church they attended, and I never inquired as to their political party preference, so I surprised myself and asked, "What church do you attend?"

"Christian Science."

My mind flew into rewind. Back to my foot injury, the doctor's prognosis, the healing, and the way my foot had taken new shape after the Christian Science Practitioner visited me.

"Please, can I go with you to your church Wednesday?" I asked. "We could still have lunch somewhere."

"Of course," she said. "I'll look forward to it."

She gave me the location of the church that coincidentally happened to be across the street from our apartment building.

She added, "See you at eleven on Wednesday."

At the appointed time, I walked over to the church, where she waited for me. We slipped into a pew as the organist played. High up on the front wall facing the congregation, in large letters were these words: "Divine Love Always Has Met and Always Will Meet Every Human Need." I liked that.

Testimonials followed the services. One-by-one, people stood to relate their healings. I glanced down at my foot and the high-heeled pump I wore. I gave thanks to God and this new interest in my life. After the services, I bought a Bible and Mary Baker Eddy's textbook, *Science and Health with Key to the Scriptures*.

Anxious to get home and read my new books, I asked Judi if we could make it a short lunch. She understood, and we planned a more leisurely lunch for the following week.

Back in our apartment I settled down on the sofa, eager to know more about Christian Science. I glanced at my watch, it was one-fifteen. Plenty of time to read, do the grocery shopping, and have dinner by six-thirty. I flipped through a few pages of the textbook, then turned to the beginning and started reading.

When I finally took my eyes away from the pages and looked up, things somehow took on a different perspective. I felt a subtle change come over me. A closeness to God I'd never felt before.

I glanced again at my watch—six o'clock. Where had the time gone? I had been reading for almost five hours. No time left to get groceries and have dinner ready. When Bill came home, I told him what happened. I hoped he would suggest going out. He did.

Bill became press agent for a play taken from the novel *The Immoralist* by Andre Gide. It starred Louis Jourdan, a handsome film star of many movies, and Geraldine Page, whom I'd seen in the play *Summer and Smoke*, where she received the New York Drama Critics Award for her performance.

Thanks to the director telling me, "Mrs. Doll, you're welcome anytime," I was able to sit in the theater during rehearsals—a real treat. I watched the actors rehearse and noticed that one of the feature players, a young man in his twenties, always stayed to himself. I never saw him speaking to others in the cast when they weren't performing. He had a shy, brooding look about him, and always seemed deep in thought. His role was that of a blackmailing homosexual Arab houseboy, and he was good.

In fact, Warner Brothers gave him a screen test because of his brilliant performance. He later became a big star and was nominated for an Academy Award as best actor in two of the only three films he made. It was unfortunate he met an untimely death, but the world would know of James Dean.

Bill surprised me for some time by not drinking. He told me he could handle it without AA. He had been sober for six months and returned to his old self again. We had been married for four years. He assured me his drinking days were behind him, and we began to talk about having a baby. I wanted so much to have a little girl, thinking she might want to dance like her mamma. A child's sex couldn't be determined then, but it didn't matter, as long as our baby was healthy. It seemed to be a good time to have one since Bill's drinking days appeared to be over.

With my mindset on a baby, it wasn't long before I became pregnant. I phoned the family to tell them. When Bill came home that night, I told him, and we went out to celebrate. The next morning I was so nauseous I couldn't get out of bed. I felt that way for the next three months. How did I get myself into all this? After that, going out was always a gamble, but I carried a paper bag in my purse, just in case.

After four months, I felt better. My craving for a quart of chocolate ice cream every day added more pounds than the doctor advised. All in all I gained forty pounds, but I was happy. Two friends, Jacqueline Susann and Joyce Matthews, gave me a baby shower. Everything I received was pink—ruffles, ribbons, all girl things.

"We just know it's going to be a petite little girl, Caren," they kept telling me. So I busied myself decorating the nursery accordingly.

Mother flew to New York to be with me for the birth of her grandchild. One evening, soon after her arrival, she timed my labor pains, and a short time later she told Bill, "It's time to get her to the hospital. Call the doctor and get a cab. We'd better leave now."

At ten o'clock, as far as I was concerned, birth didn't seem that close. I felt good and full of energy. I know if my mother hadn't been there I would have put it off for a while.

Six and a half hours later I gave birth. I heard a baby cry, and the doctor said, "Caren, you have a beautiful, healthy, baby boy."

At twenty inches long, he weighed eight pounds. One of the nurses remarked, "He must have had you, you couldn't possibly have had him!"

I will never forget the feeling when the nurse put him into my arms for the first time. He was even bigger than I expected. Then I looked down at that adorable little face and wondered why I thought having a girl was so important to me. I had a dear little boy—a future man. I didn't realize then what a blessing he would be to me in the years to come.

My friends who visited me couldn't believe I didn't have a girl. They seemed to think that just because I was petite, I'd have a little daughter. Now all the baby gifts would have to be exchanged for blue things.

We didn't even have a boy's name picked out. To help, a nurse brought us a book full of boys' names, and what each name meant. She said, "If you don't pick out a name before you leave, you'll have to go down to City Hall later."

I looked at all the possibilities. One of them caught my eye. "Jonathan. A Gift From God." That was it, if Bill approved. I chose Charles for a middle name, according to the book, "A Strong Man." I waited for Bill's choices.

He arrived drunk.

A nurse whispered to me, "Don't be upset. All fathers get plastered when they celebrate the birth of their son."

Little did she know.

During the previous months, Bill had an occasional drink but never drank to excess like before. It couldn't have happened at a more inappropriate time. I was devastated.

We brought little Jonathan home a week later with a young nurse who came highly recommended. We felt secure knowing when we were out for the evenings that our baby would be well taken care of. I learned much about caring for babies from her. I wanted to be a good mother to Jonathan.

She stayed with us for three months, then I took full charge of our son. That first evening I put him down in his crib, I felt the urge to talk to him. He was only three months old, but I had the feeling he'd know what I was saying. I learned later how important this is, so I didn't talk baby talk to him, I spoke to him as I would to an adult. "Jonathan, honey, I would appreciate it if you would sleep through the night and not want your bottle until six in the morning. Your nurse told me you wake up every morning around three or four for your bottle. It would mean a lot to me if I could get a good night's sleep until six. Would you try to do this for me, please? I love you so much." I kissed him goodnight and joined Bill in the next bedroom.

I slept soundly until I heard him crying for his bottle. I looked at the clock on the nightstand. The hands pointed to six o'clock. He had slept through the night as I had asked. I knew then that I had a remarkable child. I brought him his bottle, and he took it as I held him in my arms. I looked down at his little face, "Thank you, Jonathan."

Bill now had a large office on 150 W. 52nd St., known as Bill Doll & Co. Hanging on the wall was a huge poster-sized photo of Mike Todd that he had autographed: "To Bill, you made me what I am today but I still like you."

Mike had been Bill's client for many years, and was now producing *Around the World in 80 Days*. In this movie, Mike had cast Hollywood stars in what he called "cameo parts." David Niven, with whom we often dined, starred in the movie. He was a real charmer as well as a fine actor.

Before the opening of Mike's picture in Florida, Bill did some advance publicity in Miami. Mike was there with Elizabeth Taylor and had hired a yacht for a romantic evening to cruise down the waterways under a full moon. Bill and I stood where the boat was docked at our hotel. It was a cool night, and Elizabeth had forgotten to bring her sweater. Instead of sending someone to the room to retrieve it, Mike simply ran to the hotel's boutique and bought her a new one. They climbed aboard and sailed into the moonlight while we waved goodbye. It had been a romantic scene right out of a movie.

*Around the World* was a smash hit wherever it opened. When it appeared in Hollywood, all three of us took the train to California. It was an opportunity for Jonathan to spend time with his grandparents, who adored him. After the opening, Mike threw a party at the Beverly Hilton Hotel—and what a party! There was an Around the World buffet featuring dishes from England, France, Spain, Japan, India and, of course, those from our own country. Bill had thoughtfully arranged a table large enough to include our whole family. It had been a great evening, a nice trip, and a special treat seeing all the family together. There was already talk of Mike's film winning the Academy Award for Best Picture. A few days later, we left for New York.

As expected, the film was nominated for an Oscar. We returned to California for the awards that would be held at the Pantages Theater on Hollywood Boulevard. While Bill was somewhere in the theater conducting business, I was sitting in my seat when they announced: "And the Oscar for best picture goes to . . . *Around the World in 80 Days.*"

It was an exciting moment for Mike, and all of us. But where was Bill? I wanted him to be there with me. After it was all over and we were standing in the lobby, Bill came staggering up to us—drunk. This was the last night in the world he would have wanted to be seen like that. I wondered when he'd realize he needed help. After that fiasco, Bill stayed sober for awhile, totally convinced it wouldn't happen again. I had no idea how long it would last, but I wanted to enjoy him while I could.

One of his clients, showman Billy Rose, would often have us

spend a weekend at his Mt. Kisco estate in New York. On various fun-filled weekends, I had met actor Louis Jourdan, comedian Phil Silvers, writer Jacqueline Susann, publisher Deems Taylor, actress Geraldine Page, artist Al Hirschfeld, and a host of others. Billy's chauffeur-driven limo picked us up at our apartment on a Friday afternoon and drove us home Sunday evening.

Ever the ideal host, Billy told everyone before retiring for the night, "Whenever you decide to come down for breakfast, just tell the cook what you want." After that, we were free to read, walk around the sumptuous grounds, hang around the pool, or whatever.

They served a beautiful lunch by the Roman pool, located at the end of a huge lawn that sloped away from the house. The butler would wheel a cart down to us. Billy only asked that we be in the dining room promptly at seven for dinner.

In this wonderful atmosphere, we would never have guessed that a short time later a fire would consume Billy's beautiful estate. Although valuable paintings had been lost in that fire, we heard later that the firemen saved the television sets.

After fire destroyed Mt. Kisco, Billy purchased a small island that included a beautiful home off the coast of Connecticut. He invited Bill and me to spend a weekend with him, "And bring Jonathan, too," he said. Billy had been with us and Jonathan several times before and had been impressed by Jonathan's charm and good manners.

One Saturday morning Billy's chauffeur picked us up in the Rolls and drove us several blocks away to Billy's lavish home on East 93rd Street where Billy met us. Minutes later we were all on the road for the two-hour drive to Connecticut.

The chauffeur drove the entire way in the slow-moving right-hand lane. Billy explained, "I don't like driving in the left lane. It's dangerous facing all that oncoming traffic."

When we arrived at the seaside dock, Billy's caretaker took us by motorboat the short distance to the island. In minutes we arrived at Billy's dock by the house. Two seagulls basked in the sun on a stretch of beach. On the grounds, several peacocks roamed freely, spreading their wings and showing us their brilliant purple and blue feathers. What a breathtaking and beautiful scene. I just stood there for a while drinking it all in.

After lunch, Billy turned to Jonathan, "If you and your father would like to take a boat ride, take that little pedal-pusher over there on the sand. All you have to do is push the pedals to make it go."

"Thanks, Mr. Rose," Jonathan said, as he grabbed Bill by the hand. "Come on, Dad."

Billy and I watched them until they paddled out of sight. It would take them awhile to circle the four-acre island. As we waited for their return, we sat on the large porch, chatted and sipped a cool drink.

I thought, as I looked out to sea, it doesn't get much better than this.

The restful weekend ended too soon. Billy told us, "Anytime you two want to get away for a few days, just leave Jonathan with me. I'd love to have him."

And I knew he meant it. I had heard some unkind things said about Billy, but I tried never to judge people by what others had said. I believed Billy to be a sweet, caring little man, only inches taller than me. He wasn't handsome, but he was very smart. When Billy was only nineteen, he was the fastest shorthand stenographer in the country. He had also written the lyrics to many well-known songs, such as "It's Only a Paper Moon," "Barney Google," and "Me and My Shadow," which happened to be one of my favorite tap numbers.

I never knew Billy's previous wives, Fanny Brice, portrayed by Barbra Streisand in the movie *Funny Girl*, or Eleanor Holms, the swimming star. But I did meet Joyce Matthews, who later became my friend. I discovered she had also attended Hollywood High. I'm sure she must have been one of the beautiful girls I had seen in the quad as I looked down from the upstairs class window.

I remember when I first came to New York; a date took me to a nightclub called Billy Rose's Diamond Horseshoe. At the time, I hadn't met Billy. I loved watching the show with all the gorgeous girls strutting around in their costumes of feathers, sequins, and beads. I wished I might be one of them. But they were all a good foot taller than I was and had to be beautiful—not "cute."

# Chapter Sixteen

Gypsy Rose Lee will always be remembered as a stripper and while I never had the opportunity to see her perform, I'd heard she had a class act. She was a tall, stately lady, and any time I stood near her, I felt like a little Munchkin. One evening Gypsy invited us to a dinner party at her home. Bill had known her from a Mike Todd show, *Star and Garter*, years before I went to New York.

Several round tables had been beautifully set. Each centerpiece consisted of three tiers about a foot high, with fresh-cut flowers and white porcelain cups, each containing a votive candle. The candles nestled in the flowers created a beautifully romantic effect. I wanted to ask Gypsy where she found them, but I hesitated, since some hostesses don't like to give away recipes or party secrets. After dinner, I decided to ask anyway. She was very gracious, and beamed down at me as she told me about the Madison Avenue florist shop where she purchased them. The next day, I brought one home.

I remember the first time I ever saw a stripper. It was during the out-of-town tryout, in Boston, for *Heaven on Earth*. Some of the cast was going to the Old Howard, a well-known burlesque theater where many famous comedians got their first start.

That night at the Old Howard, the show presented girls who

stripped down to their G-strings. They then paraded back and forth across the stage, bouncing to the sensuous wail of a saxophone.

Bill had told me that there used to be a theater in New York where the girls stripped down and didn't even wear a G-string. They ended up completely nude. The police had threatened to close the place down unless they wore G-strings the next night. The following evening, the girls came out, wearing their G-strings—made of black fur. The effect was what you might imagine, but the police could do nothing about it. The G-strings were properly in place.

Basil Rathbone and his wife, screenwriter Ouida, came into our lives. She had written a three-act play for her husband and wanted Bill to produce it. Basil Rathbone as Sherlock Holmes? A role he'd made famous in film? And with Thomas Gomez as professor Moriarty—we thought, how could it miss? We have a hit here. Bill now would not only be a press agent, he would be the producer of a Broadway show.

Roles were cast and Bill hired one of the best set and costume designers as well as lighting, Stewart Chaney. The play was staged by Reginald Denham. The details of Holmes library were exact, even to the brass spittoon. We were excited opening night at the New Century Theatre. When the curtain rose, there was a round of applause.

Watching the performance from my seat, I wondered what happened to the play. It looked so good in script form, but this evening, on stage, the dialogue dragged and was frankly boring. After poor reviews we closed after only three performances. All that effort; all that money, all down the drain. But again, that's showbiz.

One day, Bill got me a ticket for a Wednesday matinee. Jason Robards was starring in *Toys in the Attic*, and I looked forward to seeing him again. When I was twelve years old, Jason and my sister Dorothy were in the same classes at Gardner Street School. Now he was appearing on stage, and known as one of Broadway's finest actors. When I saw him a few years earlier in Eugene O'Neill's *Long Day's Journey Into Night*, he gave a moving performance. I wanted to go backstage then and see him, but I didn't think he'd remember me.

When I returned home after the matinee, I phoned Dorothy. "Hi, Sis, do you still have that snapshot of Jason Robards when he was a little boy? If you do, please send it to me." I promised to tell her later why I wanted it. After three days, the little two-by-three snapshot arrived. There stood nine-year-old Jason in his corduroy pants and white shirt. What a good-looking boy.

Late one evening, Bill and I went to Sardi's, a popular restaurant for performers after their shows. In my purse I carried the picture of Jason that Dorothy had sent—just in case.

After we were settled at our table, in walked Jason. Seated only three tables away, I waited until he ordered a drink. I knew someone would probably be joining him, so I told Bill, "I'm going over to see Jason while he's still alone."

I excused myself and walked over to his table. I smiled, and said, "Hello, Jason." I laid the little snapshot on the table in front of him, anxiously waiting to see his reaction and asked, "Do you know this boy?"

He looked up at me, not knowing what to expect. Then he looked down at the picture. After scrutinizing it, he laughed, "For Christ's sake, where did you get this?"

"From your grammar school girlfriend, Jason."

"Dorothy." He grinned and stared at the snapshot.

"Yes, and I'm Dorothy's sister, Caren. I thought you'd get a kick out of seeing this."

He smiled, "I remember you. You were the best roller skater on the block. I used to watch you skate down Hollywood Boulevard past my street. This sure brings back memories. Give Dorothy my love."

Bill was drinking again and had no interest in AA. "I don't need to go," he kept telling me. "I can handle this myself. I've stayed sober for months before, and I can do it again."

He continued to do a good job for his clients and was considered one of the best press agents in the business. When he was sober, our life was wonderful, but when he was drinking, it was the pits. If only he had admitted that he needed help. "I can handle it," he kept saying.

I wanted to learn more about alcoholism so I could help Bill, if possible. I found an AA meeting close to our apartment and began attending several times a month. After one of the meetings, I stayed to talk to different people. I told one man how I used to have a martini waiting for my husband when he came home after work, but I stopped because one drink made him drunk.

He laughed. "Miss, I can tell you why you think one martini made him drunk. It was because that wasn't his first. It was probably his fourth or fifth. He started drinking during the day, then that one at home in the evening put him over the top. I did that myself and so have others. We all lie to cover up so we can continue to drink."

I asked him about his drinking and how he stopped. He said, "I come to these meetings three times a week. I've been sober for six years, and I still come to meetings to stay sober. If I take just one drink, I'll head downhill again. It's the first drink that we have to stay away from."

I told him that my husband felt he didn't need AA, that he could handle it himself.

The man told me, "We all have to reach what we call our low. He just hasn't reached his yet." Then he asked why I attended AA. "You should be going to Al-Anon," he said.

"What's that?"

"They're meetings for families and friends of alcoholics so they can learn how to deal with it."

After that meeting, I inquired around and found a new Al-Anon meeting place on our block. I arrived early and noticed two women were already there, one of them a tenant in our apartment building.

They told me, "Al-Anon is something new. We want to get the word out to those who need the help, like we do."

I volunteered to be one of them.

We weren't all wives of alcoholics. One of the women had an alcoholic daughter who refused to get help. Our group planned to rent a room in a midtown Manhattan building for people needing help. We agreed to each take a day there as often as we could.

I volunteered for every Wednesday, not realizing then that I would be with Al-Anon for the next five years. All that time I kept hoping that Bill would stop drinking. Letters arrived at our Al-Anon office, people asking what they could do to help their loved ones stay sober. There were so many letters I had to take them home to answer them all. In my replies, I stressed that the drinking wasn't their fault and suggested they get help for themselves by going to Al-Anon and learn what they could do. I also related some of my experiences with the drinking problem. I always signed the letters, "Caren D."

We received many letters of thanks. One typical letter read: "Thank you, Caren D., for explaining that my husband is an alcoholic. I thought I was the cause of his drinking. I'll get help from Al-Anon like you did."

Some letters told me they had received my letter just in time to keep them from committing suicide. That's how desperate some people could get, believing they were at fault or feeling so helpless. The letters just kept coming. I answered them using the typewriter in the evening before Bill came home. He knew I was with Al-Anon and thought it was good for me, still not realizing it all began because of him.

I often had long conversations on the phone in the office. If the call involved a child, I told them, "A child will usually look to see what the mother's reaction is when the father comes home drunk. If you get upset, so will your child. Your reaction is more important than the father's drinking. Try to stay calm and come to Al-Anon meetings. It will help both you and your child."

One survey reported, "There are five-million known alcoholics in this country. And for every one of them, friends, family, acquaintances, and businesses are affected in some way by their habit."

We had to get help for ourselves, even if we were not able to help the alcoholic. AA had what they called *The Big Book*, written by Bill Wilson, who was an alcoholic. His wife, Lois, founder of Al-Anon, visited one of our meetings and invited the group to their home.

When we arrived, she showed us a small room behind the house. She said, "This is where my husband wrote."

I stood there in awe.

He and his friend, Bob Smith, another alcoholic, tried to keep each other sober. The result became a powerful book for alcoholics, now read all over the world.

An evening in March 1958, Bill planned to attend an affair at the Friars Club Testimonial dinner in New York for Mike Todd, who was to receive an award as "Showman of the Year."

Mike had been on the west coast with his wife, Elizabeth Taylor. He would fly back on his plane, *The Lucky Liz*. Elizabeth, in bed with pneumonia, would be unable to go with him. Mike's biographer, Art Cohn, would be his only passenger.

The afternoon before the dinner, Jonathan and I were in his room playing when the phone rang. It was Bill, obviously upset. "Mike's plane crashed in New Mexico. He and Art were killed. Talk to you later, I have a lot of phoning to do."

What terrible news! I thought so much of Mike, and now he

passed on at the height of his career. So many good times we'd had together. I loved his attitude and recalled his saying, "I've been broke many times but never been poor."

How sad it must have been for Elizabeth, married a little more than a year. They seemed so crazy about each other. Bill took it hard too. He and Mike had been business buddies for over twenty years. Then it occurred to me that Bill would probably come home drunk again. And he did.

Mike's funeral was held in Chicago. We went by train. On the way I thought about the irony in the two plane crashes, mine and his. Mike was killed. I survived. You never know when your time will come.

Jonathan was such an enjoyable child to be with, and I felt so lucky to have him as my son. He was always so sharp, and when we spoke, our conversations sounded like two adults talking. He didn't attend kindergarten yet, but I was teaching him how to read by sounding out the letters in notes I would leave by his bed at night so he would find them in the morning.

We took him with us on our trips whenever possible, and he quickly learned how to get around in this world. We figured that in a couple of years he'd be ordering room service for us.

After kindergarten, we sent him to the Lycée Francais, a school highly recommended by my friend from *Best Foot Forward*, Nancy Walker. She sent her daughter there and told us it was the finest education a child could have.

When Jonathan went for his interview, they accepted him immediately. When he came home from his first day, he surprised me by saying, "Bon Jour, Mama." It looked like we might have a little Frenchman in our family.

When Bill told me he'd been hired to publicize Judy Garland's concert at the Palace I was thrilled. It had been eighteen years since we worked in *Girl Crazy* and I was looking forward to seeing her again. We took six-year-old Jonathan with us to sit in on the afternoon rehearsal. I had told him about Judy and was hoping he'd have a chance to meet her.

Rehearsals began—the orchestra started playing—out came Judy from the wings. She slowly crossed to center stage and stood there. The orchestra continued playing but not a note or word came forth from her. The orchestra stopped, and then started again— still no sound from Judy. Jonathan whispered, "Mom, when is she going to sing?"

I could see Judy was in deep trouble. It was obvious that she couldn't remember the lyrics. I knew there wouldn't be a chance to talk to her now. Everyone was totally involved with the way rehearsals were going. Later, when we left the theater, she was still struggling with her songs. I felt so sad for her.

That evening when Bill returned from Judy's concert at the Palace, I asked him about Judy's performance. He simply said, "The audience loved her."

Later in the year I was relieved and happy when I heard that she had lost weight, was in top form, and a smash hit at Carnegie Hall.

I had always wished her the best and hoped she'd have some happy years ahead, never dreaming that eight years later she would be gone.

Today, whenever I think of her, I see us having lunch together in the MGM commissary; both of us dressed as little Dorothy Gale in *The Wizard of Oz*.

The City Center's revival of *Porgy and Bess* opened in Washington, D.C. after its run in New York. As press agent, Bill and I rode the train there to see the opening night. I always enjoyed the train rides.

While gazing out the window as we moved through the countryside, I could see up ahead a string of men near the tracks that looked like they were digging ditches. As we approached them, I was stunned to see something I'd never seen before—a "chain gang." Men were shackled at the ankles by chains and bending over digging, while a guard stood over them with a gun. We passed them and I turned my head to look back. It was a scene right out of a movie; only this was for real. While I was recovering from that, I saw a billboard ahead. I couldn't read what it said as we passed, but there was no mistaking the three large letters: KKK. I didn't know what state we were traveling through, but that was my first visit to our nation's capitol and this California girl was shaken.

When we arrived at the station, I saw something I had never seen in my forty-two years. There were two drinking fountains, side-by-side. On one, the little sign said, "Whites." The other was for "Colored." Similar signs appeared on the restroom doors. I wouldn't have been as surprised to see this in other parts of the country, especially in the south, but in Washington, D.C., our nation's capitol? I had heard about segregation, but this was the first time I had seen it with my own eyes.

Later, in our hotel room, I told Bill, "I was so surprised to see the signs on the water fountains and restrooms at the station. Growing up in California, I never saw anything like that."

Bill said, "Honey, this may surprise you too. Our hotel is near the theater, but the cast is not permitted to stay here. They'll be staying at another hotel further away."

Most people are familiar with George Gershwin's folk opera about a man named Porgy and his doomed love for Bess. On this, the opening night, first-nighters packed the audience. Leontyne Price played the part of Bess, and when she sang "Summertime," I was near tears. Porgy, played by William Warfield, had a voice so full of feeling, it gave me goose bumps. They were both such superb artists, and I felt privileged to hear them. Cab Calloway, perfect as Sportin' Life, sang "It Ain't Necessarily So." The melodious voices of the actors reverberated through the theater, and when the play ended, they received thunderous applause. On our way back to the hotel I thought how outrageous that the cast who entertained us was not welcome at our hotel.

Bill publicized a new play that starred Cyril Ritchard. We were out of town sitting in the theatre watching the rehearsal when the manager approached us and told Bill he was wanted on the phone in the theater's office. When he returned moments later, I could tell by his expression that something terrible had happened.

He sat down beside me and took my hand. "Honey, your mother died today. The phone call was from the Todd office. They traced me here after receiving a call from Hollywood." I didn't hear what Bill said. I only knew I had to leave and find out what happened.

We left the theater and grabbed a cab for the train station to New York. How was I going to get to California? With an airline strike going on, over-booked trains made tickets impossible, but the Todd office got me a rail ticket. Three days each way on a train? It would seem like forever. But I had no choice. I told Bill I'd be gone ten days, counting six days by train. I had to depend on Bill and our housekeeper, Thelma, to take care of Jonathan.

When I arrived in Hollywood, I knew I had to be strong for Daddy. Dorothy told me, "Mother's death was a shocking blow to everyone, especially Daddy. He had taken her to the dentist to have a tooth pulled. He waited for her in the outer office. It took an unusually long time. Finally, the shocking news was broken to Daddy; Mother had died in the dentist's chair from a drug that affected her heart."

She'd suffered a heart attack a couple of years earlier and hadn't been her strong self since. Still, it hadn't prepared us for this traumatic news.

I always hoped my plane crash hadn't weakened her heart. She had waited hours for the long overdue plane. Finally, she cornered an attendant and insisted on knowing why the plane hadn't arrived.

Without asking her to sit down or guiding her arm to help her, the employee simply replied, "The plane crashed. There are no survivors."

It is a wonder her heart didn't fail her right then. Until she received the call from that kind man I saw on the mountain, she didn't know I survived.

Daddy had collapsed upon hearing about Mother's death. After almost fifty years of marriage, the shock was almost too much for him. He remained inconsolable. He needed someone to be with him and give him support. Dorothy had the responsibility for her two little sons, and since I was already there, I felt I should stay. I phoned Bill and told him I'd remain with Daddy a little longer, at least until we could find someone else to help him.

Bill agreed, and told me, "Stay as long as you think you should. Everything is fine here. Jonathan is doing great. He thinks you're out there to visit Grammy and Papa."

I stayed several days, then several more. I could tell my being there comforted Daddy. But he also realized that I needed to return to New York and be with my family. Three more weeks passed, and I found a woman who would cook and care for Daddy until he felt able to carry on with his life. I made the three-day train trip once more after being away one month.

After twenty-three years, my sister Dorothy's marriage ended. We asked her to come to New York for a visit. As luck would have it, a transit strike began shortly after her arrival. There was no transportation—except for automobiles. And practically no one drove a car in Manhattan if they could help it. During the strike, we had seats for a show one night and dinner reservations before the show. Dorothy and I had planned to meet Bill downtown at Sardi's restaurant, thirty blocks away from our apartment.

I told Dorothy, "Nothing is going to spoil our evening. Let's just stand on a curb, and maybe some kind soul will give us a ride."

We both dressed well for the evening and walked the short distance to Lexington Avenue where the one-way traffic faced downtown. There were no cabs in sight, no horns honking, and very few cars. We stood by the curb, and smiled. We looked like two gracious ladies desperately in need of a ride. Several cars passed without stopping.

Then a black limousine slowed down, then stopped. The chauffeur called out to us, "Where are you going, ladies?"

"Sardi's on West 44th Street," I answered.

"Hop in," he said, and opened the door for us. "I'm on my way to Las Vegas."

New York to Las Vegas? As we settled in the back seat, we noticed large fruit baskets wrapped in cellophane covered the floor around us, each tied off with a large satin ribbon. We had fun all the way downtown speculating on who'd receive those; Frank Sinatra maybe? Could this be his chauffeur?

We pulled up in front of the restaurant, and the doorman opened the door for us. We thanked the driver for the ride. He responded that he was going in that direction anyway and was glad to be of service. He wouldn't take any money—just said, "Have a nice evening," and drove off.

Dorothy could hardly wait to tell her friends back home about her limo ride to Sardi's.

# Chapter Seventeen

Summers in New York can be hot and sticky. One particularly bad one had tourists clogging the arteries of the city like bad cholesterol. Bill traveled with a one-man show. Jonathan was off to his first summer camp in Maine for eight weeks, away from the sizzling streets. If Bill hadn't been off on business, we would have vacationed in Atlantic City to keep cool. We'd been there so many times. On one occasion Bill and Joan Crawford were there to judge the Miss America contest.

Steel Pier was one of Bill's accounts. I would take Jonathan on the Atlantic City bus and we'd spend weeks enjoying the beach and the Boardwalk. Bill would join us on weekends and we'd spend happy evenings on the pier, often watching the show with the diving horse.

I remember one summer when we arrived in Atlantic City people were standing around in groups talking—some crying. I approached a tearful woman and asked, "What's going on—what happened?" She answered with a sob, "We just got news that Marilyn Monroe was found dead." I haven't forgotten that trip, and the sad fact that an icon in the movie world had passed on.

Now with Bill on the road and Jonathan at camp, I knew I

wouldn't be relishing the steamed clams at Hackney's; or the saltwater taffy on the Boardwalk. I'd miss Atlantic City.

A friend called to ask, "Since Bill is on the road and Jonathan's at camp, why don't you join us on a trip to St. Thomas for two weeks? You don't want to stay in this hot city by yourself, do you?"

I told her I really didn't mind that much.

But she insisted. "Well, we're leaving, and you're coming with us."

It sounded good, but it meant flying. I hadn't the nerve to get into an airplane since my accident in 1949, fourteen years earlier. I wasn't sure how I would react, especially on that approach to a landing.

I said, "I'd better stay here."

She continued to talk about the trip, the fun we could have visiting friends who lived there, the swimming, cool days and balmy evenings. She was getting to me. I knew I'd have to overcome this fear of flying some time. What better time than now?

We had an uneventful flight out of New York, and it remained nice all the way to St. Thomas. On the final approach to the island, I grew apprehensive. I remembered the little Ercoupe, and how much I had enjoyed flying it. But that didn't seem to help much. My mouth was dry as we approached the runway. I had a firm grip on the armrests before I felt the wheels touching solid ground. When I realized we safely landed, I began to relax. I had conquered my fears.

I spent a glorious two weeks, swimming in the crystal-clear bay, learning how to water ski, and just being with good friends. Yes, it had been a tense few moments before the landing but worth it. I had broken the spell. I knew I would fly again.

Maurice Chevalier, one of Bill's clients, performed in a one-man show on Broadway. Before the show, Bill took Jonathan and me backstage to meet the talented French actor. When we arrived at Mr. Chevalier's dressing room, we were introduced to this charming gentleman.

Jonathan began speaking French, thanks to his education at Lycée Francais. All I could catch was, "I'm happy to meet you." Mr. Chevalier appeared surprised but obviously delighted. The two of them soon held a conversation in French. Minutes later, Chevalier turned to Bill and said, "He is wonderful. He speaks like a French boy."

In 1964, we headed to the New York World's Fair. Bill had been hired to publicize the Spanish Pavilion. About three or four nights a week, we would take a party of columnists and newspaper people to the Pavilion for dinner. One evening we invited Ed Sullivan and his wife. I had always enjoyed Ed's television show and looked forward to meeting him and his wife. They raved about the Spanish food at the Pavilion as Bill hoped they would.

Publicity was the name of the game, and I was learning more about the game, and what a public relations man could do for a client. Bill never liked being called a public relations man. He always preferred to be known as a press agent. "That's what I am," he'd say.

I learned more about his business that night, and also discovered "Sangria," a drink they served in a pitcher that looked like fruit punch—and, in fact, packed a "punch."

Bill didn't drink that night. Good for him!

Federico Fellini, the Italian director, hired Bill for his next movie, *Juliet of the Spirits*. It starred Fellini's wife, Giulietta Masina. For Federico's first color feature film, he wanted the New York publicity.

In September 1965, Bill and I flew to Rome for three days. I wasn't all that enthused about the long flight over water, but after the St. Thomas trip, I felt better about flying.

Bill said, "After Rome, we'll go to Zurich to see John Ringling North," another of his clients. "Then we'll see Paris and London."

Sounded wonderful—my first trip to Europe.

The reviews of Fellini's pictures had mentioned surrealism and symbolism being the basis for his stories—so different from our

American films. I had seen only two of his movies. *La Dolce Vita*, starring Marcello Mastroianni and Anita Ekberg that won the Grand Prize at the Cannes Film Festival. Who could forget that scene in the Trevi Fountain? The other starred his wife, Giulietta Masina, *La Strada*, which won an Oscar for Best Foreign Film.

We flew all night, and at seven in the morning we had a glimpse of land up ahead. From my window seat there below us lay the familiar "boot" of Italy exactly as I remembered from the pictures in my school geography books. We grabbed a cab to the Excelsior Hotel on the Via Veneto. Here, the streets were jammed with motorcycles, and little Fiats looked like oversized bugs scurrying here and there. The room wouldn't be available until that afternoon. Bill had planned to be in Rome a day ahead of the meeting so we could sleep off our jet lag. So much for that plan. We ate a quick breakfast, then toured the Vatican. I was so sleepy I could hardly keep my eyes open.

At three o'clock, we hurried back to the hotel, fell on the bed, and slept. We awoke at seven, ordered dinner from room service, then slept again through the night.

Freshly rested, we looked forward to the new day. At ten o'clock, we received a call from the lobby that the studio car had arrived. We were whisked off to meet director Federico Fellini.

He was a big man, and it surprised me to hear such a soft, gentle voice greeting us. I had expected a brusquer manner from a man his size. After he greeted Bill, he turned to me and said, "Hello, Mrs. Doll, darling." From that moment on, every time he spoke to me it started with, "Mrs. Doll, darling."

He showed us around the studio, all the while talking to Bill about the movie. He had based the film on his wife, Guilietta, who he said had been his inspiration for the film. During the studio lunch, several others connected with the movie joined us. The group spoke English, as well as Italian.

Fellini screened his movie, *Juliet of the Spirits*, for us. His wife showed the same remarkable expressions of joy, sadness and amazement on the screen in this movie as she had in *La Strada*. I hoped I'd have a chance to meet her before we left Rome.

After the screening, we returned to the Excelsior, changed clothes for the evening, enjoyed a delicious dinner in the hotel, then spent the evening sitting on the Via Veneto—people watching.

The next morning we visited the Catacombs where I almost lost Bill in that labyrinth of caves and tunnels. We walked on the Via Veneto, had lunch with an Italian newspaperman whose name I don't remember. We shopped at Dal-Co, where they took an imprint of my feet, showed me leather and styles of shoes I could order, and said they'd ship them to New York for me when they were finished. I ordered pumps in black alligator and wore them for years. They were beautifully made and lasted longer than any pair I'd ever had.

Evening came all too fast. Where had the day gone? We dined at Capretzio's, and then met Fellini in the hotel bar. After drinks he took us to meet his wife, Giulietta, and friends in the hotel suite where they were staying.

Fellini towered over Giulietta, like Bill towered over me. I liked her immediately. We had a wonderful evening together. When we said our goodbyes, Fellini walked us to the door and said, "Ciao, Mrs. Doll, darling."

We flew Swissair to Zurich the next morning to see Mr. North. For the past several years, Bill had been press agent for Ringling Brothers and Barnum & Bailey Circus when it appeared in Madison Square Garden. Mr. North's chauffeur met us at the airport, and I enjoyed the two-and-a-half-hour scenic ride to reach Mr. North's villa—rich colorful flowers lined the highway to Zurich.

Mr. North greeted us, and we spent the afternoon talking business. He insisted I call him John. Listening to his discussions with

Bill, I learned much about the operation and management of a circus—a fascinating business, and a facet of the circus I had never even considered when growing up.

Every year, Ringling Brothers and Barnum & Bailey Circus appeared in New York's Madison Square Garden. Publicized as "The Greatest Show on Earth," I'd never seen a three-ring circus like this before.

As a child I had seen a circus in a huge tent when it came to Los Angeles, but it had only one ring where all the entertainment took place. In New York, each of the three-rings contained entertainment so fascinating that you didn't know where to look next. Lions and trainers were in one ring, dancing ponies in another. Elephants balancing on their hind legs in still another. They left the rings and more circus entertainers entered, including everyone's favorite, the clowns. So much going on. Easy to understand why a parent might say to a child, "Your room looks like a three-ring circus."

We sometimes took Jonathan to an afternoon performance. I loved watching him more than watching the performers: the way his face lit up as the clowns bounced out into the arena; his laughter as they tumbled out of a small automobile obviously too small to hold them all; the anxious expression as the lion tamer put the animals through their paces, and how intense he was as his favorites, the daring high wire performers, balancing precariously above the sawdust, sometimes without a net. What an enjoyable experience—watching the circus through the eyes of a child.

When Bill went to the rehearsals in Madison Square Garden, I sometimes accompanied him, where I had the opportunity to meet several of the trapeze artists and animal trainers. The whole area smelled of sawdust and animals, with the crew scurrying around and the artists in work clothes. The scene reminded me of some of the movie sets I'd worked on.

Then opening night arrived. Although a far cry from an opening night at the theater, similarities did exist. Many in the audience dressed for the occasion with glitz and glamour.

After the show, many of New York's "first-nighters" went to a beautiful party at the Garden. In the center of each gala table sat a bowl of Beluga caviar. The tiny plump eggs just waited to be eaten— and I did enjoy them.

After our combined business and social meeting with John, we rode back to the Ascot Hotel in Zurich. We arrived about midnight, ready for some much needed sleep before flying on to Paris the next morning.

In Paris, we checked in at the Lancaster, a French hotel not often frequented by tourists. From the beautiful bedroom suite, a door opened up to a garden. I was sorry I couldn't speak French like our son Jonathan. That's all we heard in the hotel, and my English seemed out of place even though they understood English.

We had a marvelous evening dining at Maxim's. What impressed me were the beautiful women at the tables—they all had such a lovely glow. After dinner when I took out my lipstick and looked into my compact mirror, I saw that same glow, and thought I looked as beautiful as the others. Even Bill had noticed. We finally figured it out. They lit every table with a pink shade. I don't recall if it was a candle or a bulb inside, but the pink from the lamp cast that flattering light.

We ended the evening at the Lido, a large Parisian cabaret that featured dancers and other entertainment.

The next three days in Paris, we shopped, rode through Montemarte, took a tour through Versailles, dined at La Tour d'Argent, saw the Follies Bergere, and the Moulin Rouge. We didn't do the Eiffel Tower. That would have to wait for another time. We arrived in London via British European Airways and checked in at the

Dorchester Hotel. After dinner, we took in a revue at the Hippo-
drome Theater restaurant.

The next morning after breakfast, we rented a car and driver, who
showed us much of the countryside and other local attractions in
the three days we had left of our trip. While very beautiful, the cold,
damp, sunless weather didn't impress me. We visited Piccadilly Circus, Trafalgar Square, the Tower of London, witnessed the changing
of the guard, Buckingham Palace, and Westminster Abbey.

Our driver took us to the Mitre Hotel in Hampton Court in
Middlesex where we had lunch. We entered Henry VIII's great
kitchen in Hampton Court Palace that was large enough for ballroom dancing if there had been a proper floor. One of Henry's many
wives might have ordered her last supper from this center of epicu-
rean delights.

That evening, we saw a show at the London Palladium, a min-
strel show at the Victoria Palace, and ended with a leisurely ride
through Soho before returning to our hotel.

On our last day in London, it seemed only proper to have a "spot
of tea," as they say. They served us in the hotel lobby, while we sat in
soft comfortable chairs. The tea came complete with scones, butter
and crumpets. Typically English.

Daddy would have enjoyed all this, since he was born in London.
He didn't arrive in the United States until he was in his late teens,
but I remember Mother had prepared his pot of tea and cookies or
biscuits every afternoon.

We left London on Pan-American at six-thirty at night and arrived in New York a few hours later. It had been a wonderful trip,
and we were happy to be back home with our son.

# Chapter Eighteen

After our whirlwind tour of Europe, we planned another train trip to California with Jonathan. He had traveled so many times with us on the *20th Century*, and the *Super* Chief, that when we entered the dining cars, the waiters greeted him by name.

Away from all the hectic schedules and business dealings, I knew that at some point Bill would start drinking again. And he did. He would get drunk, and apologize the next day. This pattern continued until almost time to return to New York. I had learned from Al-Anon that it doesn't get better without help, it only gets worse. The thought of returning to the east coast with him and waiting anxiously every evening to see if he would come home drunk or sober took its toll on me. If he would only seek help, like others I knew who had sobered up, I would have continued to support him. He assured me he could handle it. Would he ever admit that he couldn't? My friend and her husband had been going to AA since she discovered, at that first meeting, that she was an alcoholic too. They both stayed sober. If only I could have gotten Bill to go.

Strangely enough, the neighbor, who took us to that first meeting, had fallen down while drunk and broken her hip. She stopped going to meetings after twelve years of sobriety. She didn't think she needed AA anymore. Then she took a drink, got drunk, and continued drinking. That really shocked me.

I decided not to return to New York with Bill this time. Jonathan and I would stay in California for a while longer. I realized how much his drinking had affected me. Every afternoon my stomach would start churning as I guessed if he'd be coming home drunk, or sober that night. I didn't think I could continue much longer. Al-Anon had helped me but not enough to continue living that way. I loved him, and he loved me, but it became unbearable seeing him destroy himself.

It even affected Jonathan, who was then age nine. When I told him we weren't going right back to New York, he said to me, "Mom, won't it be a relief not to have to worry if Dad's going to come home drunk?"

That really did it. The next morning Bill returned to New York without us. Bill and I had separated for two weeks several years prior, and he promised he'd stop drinking. We reunited again for a while, and it was wonderful. Then he came home drunk. Back in New York, we talked at length about his problem. He believed he could handle his addiction without help. With this attitude, our marriage could no longer survive. After sixteen years, I needed peace for Jonathan and for me.

Bill moved into the New York Athletic Club where he was a member. Jonathan had been at the Lycée Francais for five years, and although he spoke French fluently and had a wonderful scholastic foundation, the advanced classes had become difficult for him. I felt the need for a change.

I accepted an invitation from a friend to visit her in Palm Beach, Florida. Jonathan stayed in school in New York with Thelma, who had been with us since he was eight months old.

While in Palm Beach, I noticed the public junior high school nearby. The beach and the palm trees reminded me of Southern California. I thought it would be nice if Jonathan could enjoy the same lifestyle that I had growing up.

I had an idea. Why not sublet our New York apartment furnished and find a small furnished place in Palm Beach? We could start over. I had some beautiful memories of New York, but others were not so beautiful. We wouldn't have the luxuries we'd had there, but our peace of mind seemed to be more important at this time. I knew Jonathan would be overjoyed at the thought of living this new lifestyle. Our trips to California always made him so happy.

I had returned to New York when I received a call from an actress friend. "Are you familiar with French actress Genevieve?" she asked. "She's on the Jack Paar show. We're friends, and she's going to star in the musical *Can Can* this summer up on Cape Cod. She'll be playing in several towns and is looking for a companion to be with her on the tour. Her husband will join her on weekends. I thought you might be interested."

"Yes," I said, without hesitation.

We set an appointment, and Jonathan went along with me. Genevieve, a beautiful French woman with a delightful accent, greeted us warmly and invited us into her home. We discussed the details of the tour. I would drive her car, have coffee ready in the morning, and help her with her costumes. In each town, we'd be living in a house with a pool. Being a "companion" sounded like the ideal job. I'd never done anything like that before, and the money would help.

While we talked, Jonathan sat quietly nearby. When Genevieve smiled at him, he began talking to her in French. She appeared as surprised as Maurice Chevalier had been, and, in the middle of their conversation, jumped up, "Oh, Jonathan must come with us. He'll love my dog, Poodie."

We settled that on the spot. I'd been hoping that would happen.

When the tour ended, Genevieve gave me a bonus. "This is for your new lifestyle in Florida."

She surprised me further with a pink, full-length, silk chiffon stole, edged all around with pink ostrich feathers that she had worn in one of her scenes. I put it around my shoulders, and it reached my ankles. The memories of the red ostrich feathers at my sixteenth birthday made me feel young again. What goes around comes around.

Once back in New York, I concentrated on subletting our apartment. We soon had a tenant, and my friend in Palm Beach found us a small furnished apartment near her.

Bill continued to drink, but he had seen so little of Jonathan, we might as well be gone.

Our dear housekeeper, Thelma, who had lived with us for twelve years, couldn't come with us. What a shame that because of the bottle, so many lives changed.

All that was left of the plane crash near Chatsworth, California, July 12, 1949.

My photo in the hospital appeared in many newspapers across the country.

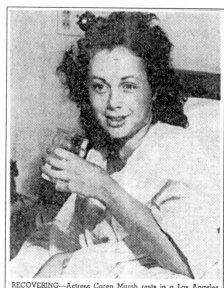

RECOVERING----Actress Caren Marsh rests in a Los Angeles hospital after receiving a mangled foot and extreme shock in the Chatsworth plane crash.

(Acme Photo)

Letter from Bing Crosby after the crash.

# Starlet in Air Disaster Tells How Life Was Saved

(Editor's Note: Film and television starlet Caren Marsh, flying to Hollywood, was one of the injured in Tuesday's plane crash near Chatsworth, Calif. She tells of the tragedy in the following dispatch.)

## By CAREN MARSH
As Told to United Press

HOLLYWOOD, July 13. (U.P.) A woman I'll probably never see again saved my life when our plane crashed as we were coming in for a landing.

I don't know who the woman passenger is but I hope I can find her to thank her for saving me from a horrible cremation death. I don't think I would have got out alive without her help.

I'm lucky to be here in Cedars of Lebanon Hospital even though my leg is mangled.

The flight from New York had been pleasant all the way except for the last hour. Then two passengers started a fight. I was dozing at the time but others told me it just lasted a few seconds and wasn't as good as some of the Hollywood nightclub battles.

That was just about an hour before the crash.

The last thing I remember was flying through fleecy, white clouds. I thought we were preparing to land. Then there was a deafening roar.

I heard screams and fire crackling. I was dazed. It was like a bad dream. My legs hurt and I felt numb.

"Let's get the Hell out of here," a woman said to me. She grabbed my arm and dragged me from the flames. She was wonderful. I don't know who she was and couldn't recognize her if I saw her.

I shudder to think what would have happened to me if she hadn't been there. The bad dream ended happily for me because of her.

Back to ballet instructor, Theodore Kosloff, to
strengthen legs after the crash. February 1950.

At the El Rancho Vegas pool.

Jason Robards in grammar school.

Christmas, 1950. Three months married.

Modeling a portable beach cabana
for one of Bill's clients.

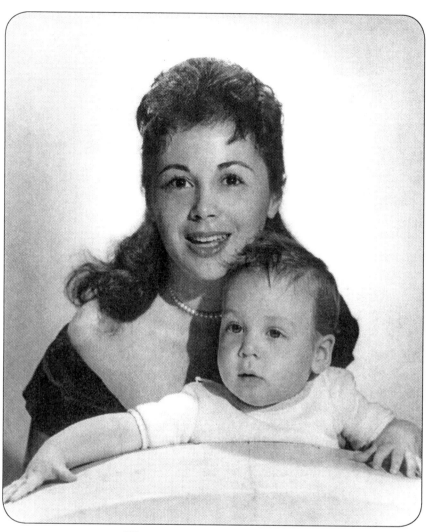

With eight-month-old Jonathan.

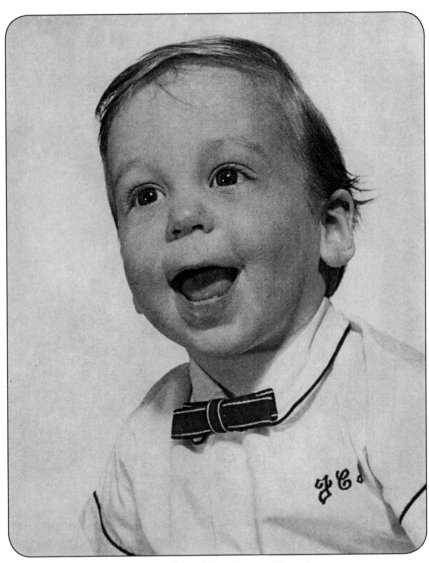

One-year-old birthday photo of Jonathan.

Four-year-old Jonathan
in Atlantic City.

Eight years
old with Bill at
summer camp.

Jonathan, the aspiring radio DJ at six.

The annual toy fair at the Hotel New Yorker. Displaying some of Bill's clients' toys with Beverly Dennis.

Bill and I with Federico
Fellini in Rome.

With John Ringling North
in Zurich, Switzerland.

Federico Fellini and his wife, actress Giulietta Masina.

At Dorothy's condo in
Ft. Lauderdale, Florida.

Sunning at
Dorothy's North
Hollywood Home.

My dance studio in Florida.

# Chapter Nineteen

The night before we left for Florida, New York became practically paralyzed by a blizzard. The weather man said the storm would last all night. The lease in Palm Beach had been signed, and our new tenant in New York prepared to move in. We couldn't change our plans. Good weather or bad weather we had to leave.

The following morning the blizzard slacked off. Snow piled up on the sidewalks as the streets were being cleared, but there was no cab in sight to take me to the car rental garage. I stood on a corner and waited for a downtown bus, then transferred in the cold at another corner and waited for a cross-town bus.

I drove the rental car back to our apartment and met Thelma and Jonathan who waited anxiously in the lobby with our luggage.

We packed the car and fought back the tears. We would miss Thelma terribly, but I couldn't afford to keep her with us. She couldn't leave anyway. She had family and grandkids in New York. We hugged and said our goodbyes. As we pulled away from the curb, I could see her in the rearview mirror waving to us from the sidewalk.

With the dismal weather, the trip south wasn't going to be the pleasant drive I had looked forward to. I drove slow and passed practically no traffic on the wet and slippery turnpike. I felt uneasy in those conditions but didn't want Jonathan to know. I decided to make a game of it.

"Pretend I'm the pilot, and you're the copilot. Look through the binoculars and tell me what the signs in the distance say. We'll fly low and slow all the way to Florida."

Two days later, we could see sunshine. After four days, we arrived in Palm Beach and moved into our little furnished, two-bedroom, bungalow apartment on Brazilian Avenue.

The next day we went to Burdine's department store in West Palm Beach and outfitted Jonathan in Levi's and shirts that the saleslady said the kids were wearing. At the Lycée Francais, the dress code had been navy blazer, gray slacks, white shirt and navy tie, which he had been wearing since he enrolled at the age of six.

Now, at twelve years old, he would be attending a public junior high, located four blocks from our new home. He couldn't believe how different school life was for him in Palm Beach. In New York, he would come home after school; have a glass of milk, then settle down at his desk with homework. Here, when school was out, the kids ran the few blocks to the beach after changing clothes at home. Jonathan was making friends fast, and so was I.

After he left for school in the mornings, I drove to the local college in West Palm Beach with a friend who suggested we take a speed writing course to help pass the time. I thought it a good idea in case I decided to take a secretarial job.

I mentioned to one of my friends that I knew Hawaiian dancing. Excitedly, she said, "Show me, Caren. It's something I've always wanted to do." I danced some of the movements and got her started. She told a friend, and that friend told another friend. The word got around quickly. I soon had a class of eight women. My first year there and I was teaching dancing in bare feet. I knew I would be at some point in time—and this must be the time. It wasn't long before

I taught Hawaiian dancing down the coast from Palm Beach to Fort Lauderdale in condos and clubs.

We were happy in Palm Beach. Jonathan was getting tan and looking healthy. I got up at six in the morning to prepare his favorite breakfast before school: fresh Florida orange juice, bacon, eggs, toast and hot chocolate with a marshmallow on top.

When he came home from classes, I made sure I was around, in case he needed to talk about school or any problems he might be having. Then off he would go with his pals. We lived a pretty carefree life.

A friend invited me to spend a day at her beach club. We lay by the pool—I in my bikini, and she pointed to a man standing nearby. "Caren, see that man over there?"

I sat up and looked.

"He's a well-known artist, and a friend of Hemingway. He asked me to find out if you'd pose for him. He does nudes and referred to you as a 'pocket-sized Venus.'"

He saw us looking his way so he walked over and introduced himself.

I told him, "I'd like to pose for you, but not nude. If I can wear my bikini, fine. If not, thank you for the compliment anyway."

Two days later, I posed while he sketched. When he finished, he gave me more money than we had agreed upon. I was a bit surprised when I saw the finished sketch of a woman in a bikini with large hips and heavy legs, looking nothing like my slim hundred-pound frame. He simply used his artist's prerogative and sketched his artistic perception. Regardless, I was happy to earn the money. It made me wonder if maybe I should consider charging for the dance lessons I had been giving for free.

Bill sent child support money on a regular basis, which I appreciated. But I knew I should get busy and earn some money myself. I thought about studying for a securities license and sell mutual funds. I had cashed my mutual funds to pay for our trip to Florida. I signed up for a course but found it hard doing the math, which had always been my weakest subject in school. When I took the test, I gritted my teeth and wanted to scream, but I passed. I got my license, signed with an office, and soon after made my first sale. But I wasn't happy. I didn't enjoy this sort of work. I would have been happier making money giving dance lessons.

I soon tired of selling mutual funds as the real estate market boomed. I thought I'd give it a try. Again I studied long hours and went through the same misery and frustration I felt when I studied for my securities license. Would I ever get the answers right? They held the test in another city. After a long drive, I faced a three-hour exam, and a long wait for the results to arrive by mail. When that day eventually arrived, I tore open the envelope and found that I had passed. I had my real estate license.

I delighted in finding homes for families. Now, instead of spending time at the beach with friends, I worked in the real estate office and researched all the information I could find on Palm Beach homes. Determined to be a success in my new profession, not only for the income, but for the satisfaction of knowing I was accomplishing something new, I worked diligently to match the clients to a certain type of home. They usually decided on the right place for them, and at the right price, after seeing only one or two listings. My first commission check was cause for celebration, and Jonathan and I dined on lobster that evening.

By word of mouth, it didn't take me long to accumulate a clientele. A New York realtor contacted me. New Yorkers, who had been to Palm Beach, told her that I was the best in the business. As a result, she sent me clients looking for a winter home. With all this business, I no longer had time to teach dance.

When I showed an "Open House," I always met interesting people. One of my clients, whose brother was a famous movie star, lived there. He invested in houses I would locate for him on the beach, or the Inter-Coastal waterway. He would redecorate them and resell the property for a handsome profit. I picked up a lot of decorating ideas from him.

I found a beautiful two-story home with an elevator, located right on the beach. The only big drawback was the outdated bath off the master bedroom, which was tiled in lavender and green. Rather than the expense of ripping out and replacing the tile, he painted the walls and used fabric for the bedroom in the same shades of lavender and green, creating a fabulous overall result. Anyone would be impressed to see the bath had been tiled to match the bedroom. A clever idea, indeed.

I received an engraved invitation from friends to attend a cocktail party at the Beach Club to meet Commander Edgar Mitchell, the astronaut from *Apollo XIV*. I arrived in a room filled with beautifully dressed women. The men wore jackets ranging in color from pink and light blue, to yellow and navy. All wore white slacks with white shoes and—in typical Palm Beach style—no socks.

The hostess introduced me to Commander Mitchell, who greeted me with a smile and a warm handshake. Never one to ask for autographs, I just had to have his. I picked up a paper cocktail napkin from a nearby table and borrowed a pen from a friend. I offered them both to Commander Mitchell with apologies for not having anything better for him to sign.

When he began to write on my little napkin, it seemed like he took more time than it should take for an autograph. He handed the napkin back to me where he had written, "To Caren, with the prettiest dress at the party." I felt good that I had bought that embroidered white lace see-through mini-dress with the flesh-colored slip. It was a winner.

Jonathan came to me one day and announced, "Mom, I'm fourteen now and I want to make some bucks. Instead of going to the beach every day after school with the kids, I want to bag groceries at Brinkley's Market. Mr. Brinkley said I could start right away, and he'll pay me a dollar-fifty an hour. If I carry groceries to the customer's cars, he said they will probably tip me a quarter."

"That's wonderful," I said, admiring his willingness to work rather than play at the beach every day.

Brinkley's was the only market in Palm Beach. It was located on County Road, a few blocks from our apartment.

On an afternoon before Christmas, Jonathan called from the market. "Mom, they have so many orders going out for Christmas Eve that Mr. Brinkley asked if I'd stay and help. I won't be late." I told him that would be fine.

Later that evening he rushed in the door waving a bill in his hand. "Mom, I delivered a Christmas order on my bike to one of the yachts moored right here at the Brazilian docks and look!" He held up a five-dollar bill. "They gave me this tip and said, 'Merry Christmas.' Isn't that great?"

Some time later, Mr. Brinkley advanced Jonathan to stock boy and gave him a twenty-five-cent an hour raise.

My sister Dorothy left California and moved to a Fort Lauderdale apartment two hours south of Palm Beach. As a single lady, she looked for a new start somewhere else. Her kids were in college and on their own. She had become a licensed massage therapist and soon had many female clients.

She told me a lot of people enjoyed dancing in Fort Lauderdale and called me one day. "The dance studios here welcome the public on weekends. Why don't you drive down here on Friday after work, have a relaxing massage, dance in the evenings, and spend the nights with me before you leave on Sunday?"

"Sounds like a great idea," I told her.

"You could do this every weekend, and it will keep you from getting stressed out."

She was right. By now, Jonathan had graduated from high school, and I would have more time for myself. I could even start dancing classes in Fort Lauderdale on the weekends. Dorothy said her clients had been begging her to have me come down there and teach. During the week, I still sold real estate in Palm Beach.

I enjoyed that weekend in Fort Lauderdale, and others after that. I discovered a lot of good dancers, many who could do a mean rumba.

I remembered what my mother once said to me many years before, "You can't rumba your way through life." She was right, but this was a different time . . . and a different life. I had missed the dancing, and life was becoming fun again.

One weekend Dorothy greeted me, saying "We're not dancing tonight, I bought theatre tickets."

"How come?" I asked.

She replied with a smile, "We're seeing a Broadway play called *That Championship Season*, and guess who's playing the lead? Jason Robards."

I knew that meant a lot to her. After all, he was her Gardner Street Grammar School boyfriend. She continued, "I sent a note to the theatre asking him if he remembered me, and could we see him backstage after the show."

That afternoon he phoned and said, "Waddya mean, 'if I remember you?' You'd better come back and see me."

When we left that night for the theatre, Dorothy was carrying a 1937 Bancroft Jr. High graduation photo. Jason was in the group, and so was Judy Garland, who had told me during our *Wizard of Oz* lunches how pleased she was to have been in that picture.

"Why are you taking this rolled up photo tonight?" I asked.

She showed me her school friends' signatures on the back and replied, "I never had a chance to get Jason's signature, so I intend to ask him for it tonight."

The show was excellent and Jason gave his usual brilliant performance. Backstage we met in his dressing room. He seemed delighted to see Dorothy after all these years and remembered the night in New York when I placed that picture of him as a child on his table at Sardi's.

Dorothy unrolled the graduation photo and asked him to sign on the back. I noticed a twinkle in his eye as he looked at her. Then, taking the photo, he wrote: "To D.M. and our kiss in the sandbox at Gardner. Love, Jason."

In church one Sunday, Jonathan and I met a nice man, a deejay who was visiting in Palm Beach. There was an immediate rapport, probably because he didn't drink. Jonathan had seen too much of that with his father. Soon after our first meeting, he invited Jonathan to go with him for the weekend to a station in Tallahassee where he used to work. When they returned, Jonathan excitedly told me, "Mom, I don't want to go to college now; I want to be in radio."

What could I say? I had told my parents I didn't want to go to college. I had my own dreams. So what could I say to Jonathan, except, "Okay, give it a try."

Jonathan moved to Tallahassee to pursue his radio career, starting out as a "gopher."

I sold real estate, but the market began to slump.

This man was romantic and determined to have me for his wife. We had a lot of good times together, riding on his motorcycle, and sailing on his boat. Everything was an adventure with him. He was a take-charge kind of fellow that I felt I needed.

At one point, Jonathan told me with a wry smile, "Mom, if you don't marry him, I will."

I finally said, "Yes," to this determined young man, and we were married.

On Thanksgiving a few months later, we rode his motorcycle across the state to the west coast of Florida. We celebrated with dinner at Naples, Florida, where we spent the night. The next morning we rode back. I felt like a teenager again without the bobby socks.

We moved out of my apartment to a condo on the waterway so my new husband could watch the boats glide by. He loved boats as much as I loved dancing.

I spent a weekend with Dorothy while he was out sailing. While there, I met a woman who was the Entertainment Director at Palm Aire, a spa in Pompano Beach. She was starting a belly dance class there and knew I was a dance instructor.

"How about Hawaiian dancing, instead?" I asked.

"No, I don't think so," she said. "Belly dancing is becoming very popular. We want to have classes at the spa. Do you teach it?"

I lied and said, "Not lately. When do you want to start these classes?"

"In three weeks. And if you want it, the job is yours." She quoted a price, gave me her card, the starting date, and said, "It's definite then."

Great. Now all I had to do was to find a teacher and learn belly dancing in three weeks. I heard there was a wonderful teacher in Fort Lauderdale who was from New York and had a fine reputation. I contacted her and explained the need for private lessons because of the timing. I started immediately and loved the music as well as the dance.

"Belly dancing is an ancient art," she began. "It's a shame it's made to look so cheap in this country."

Very quickly I learned to move my body to the sensuous rhythm of the dance. I took lessons from this beautiful lady the next three weekends and practiced every day. When I asked her for an auto-graphed photo after my last lesson, she wrote, "To my best student and future dancer, Caren. Love, Teena."

I began teaching at Palm Aire once a week—and in my bare feet. The more I practiced, the more I loved this ancient art form and could see why it was becoming so popular. I bought a beautiful costume complete with veil and discovered that the veil work was an art in itself. I added an "A" onto my name so I would be known as "Carena" professionally when belly dancing.

Project Hope was having their Harvest Jubilee Dance in Fort Lauderdale, and they hired me to perform. The honored guest was Percival Brundage, former director of the Bureau of Budget under President Eisenhower. While dancing to the strains of the exciting Middle-Eastern music, I felt a sense of joy and freedom I had never experienced before. That night I knew I would love this dance for the rest of my life.

At one of the belly dance seminars, I met Tambil, who was from Turkey and had been King Farouk's favorite dancer. We were the same size, and there was an instant rapport. A week later, I drove two hours north to her home for a private lesson, and she taught me the Turkish style of belly dancing that included the fast ribcage bounce. As I drove back to Palm Beach, I couldn't wait to put on my costume and watch the coins bounce up and down.

It wasn't long before we moved again. Being a true vagabond, my husband much preferred adventure to settling down in one commu-nity. He wanted to give up the condo and live in a motor home so we could travel. We would take off on short trips to parks and beaches, camp beside lakes, next to the ocean—anywhere. There seemed to be no limit where you could park a motor home for the night. The gas crunch caused long lines of cars at the stations. So much for living on the highways and byways of America. Accordingly, we sold the motor home and moved to a mobile home park, complete with a small lake and swans.

On one occasion, the tenants planned a luau. They intended to hire entertainers, but I had a suggestion I passed on to a neighbor. "Why don't you let me teach you and some of the other women how to do Hawaiian dancing? You wouldn't have to hire entertainers. We would all be the floorshow. I can order the grass skirts. Think how thrilled all the husbands and friends would be."

The idea went over, and we began preparations. Soon, fourteen women swayed to the strains of Hawaiian music. We rehearsed for weeks while I taught them how to move their hips, hands, and feet. None of them had ever done anything like that before, but I'd never seen a happier, more enthusiastic group. They could hardly wait for the grass skirts to arrive so they would look authentic.

The show became a huge success. Everybody likes to be in the limelight at least once in their lifetime, and these dancers were having the time of their lives. And so did the audience who watched their friends, neighbors, and spouses. One husband came up to me after the show. "I want to meet the person who put so much life in my wife." A nice compliment that made it all worthwhile.

Less than a year later, my husband was offered a job managing a condominium complex in South Palm Beach. The irresistible employment package included a free, two-bedroom ocean-front condo. Early each morning I walked along the beach and combed the shoreline for shells and colorful pieces of broken glass that had washed up during the night. I also taught some of the women in our complex how to belly dance.

Before a year was up, my husband got antsy, and we prepared to move again. He wanted to live on the west coast of Florida where he could sail his boat in the calmer waters of Tampa Bay instead of the Atlantic Ocean.

We found an apartment in St. Petersburg, and after a few months, he found an apartment he liked better. So we moved again. I hoped we had finally settled. I wanted to set up my own dance studio and found a perfect location on a corner near the yacht club, but it needed renovating. We signed a lease and began painting and decorating. I'd been teaching exercises that I had created along with the Hawaiian and belly dancing. When I had shown them to some of my students, they remarked, "What unique exercises and so beautiful." I took a clue from that and decided that's what I would call them, "Beautiful Exercises." Then I decided that's what I would call my studio and had a sign made for the building.

When I was ready to open, I first had to attract business. Again, the idea of leaflets came to mind. I had a bundle of them printed advertising my Beautiful Exercises—but this time, there was no airplane out of which to toss them. I started out on foot, dropping them off at shops and wherever else people would see them. Within a week students of all ages swamped the studio. I told them the exercises were good for anyone from the athlete to the couch potato. My dance classes filled quickly, and I was happy to be doing what I loved to do . . . and in my own studio.

While this happened, I couldn't believe that my nomad husband was thinking about our giving up the apartment to live on a houseboat or sailboat. That did it. If that's what he wants, I thought, then he should have it—but not with me. After six moves, I wasn't about to move again. The marriage ended after four years.

I was free again. I had raised a son I was proud of who lived on his own as a radio DJ since he was eighteen. My studio was doing well, and I looked out for myself, dancing and teaching from morning until night. Several of my students told me how I had changed their lives, and I felt a certain satisfaction in this.

One woman, who had taken private belly dancing lessons from

me, used to fly her own plane in the Powder Puff Derby. Then she had a heart attack and could no longer fly. After that, she fell in a deep depression. Her husband came to me one day and told me that the belly dancing lessons had literally saved her life. The dancing had brought back her *joie de vivre*, and she was soon flying around the room with veils swirling and cymbals tinkling.

The studio had done well, but expenses were high. I had no money for extras. I would have loved to go dancing but really couldn't spare the five-dollar admission fee at the local studios. Then on a Saturday afternoon I saw an ad in the paper for dancing at the YMCA for only one dollar on Saturday nights. What irony. After all the dancing I had enjoyed at such beautiful places from the Coconut Grove in Los Angeles to El Morocco in New York, I made my way to the YMCA because I could afford the dollar admission. The thought of where I had been, and where I was now, saddened me. Lonely and dejected, I began to feel sorry for myself and cried all the way to the Y. When I arrived, I managed to dry my eyes and wipe away those tears of self-pity, determined to have myself a good time.

Inside, a young, attractive couple from England taught the newest craze in dancing—Disco. John Travolta had started it all in his new 1977 movie, *Saturday Night Fever*.

I began learning those steps. What an evening it turned out to be. I had a marvelous time. All the anger, frustration, and self-pity I felt earlier were released just listening to the music and dancing to this hot, new craze. That night became the best dollar investment I ever made.

The next day, I placed a new banner in my studio window: "Disco Dancing Taught Here." I soon had a class—the oldest in her seventies, the youngest was eight years old. Thanks, YMCA! I vowed never to feel that self-pity again—you never know what wonderful surprises might be right around the corner.

While busy finding my life and spirit again, I received some sad news. A friend in New York sent me an article from the *New York Times*, dated March 4, 1979. The article headline read, "Bill Doll, Prominent Press Agent." It told of his death. Until I saw that article, I hadn't known that Bill had suffered two strokes.

A few years before when I had flown to New York to visit friends, I phoned him to say hello. He had asked me to have breakfast with him the following morning and wanted me to see Lauren Bacall in *Applause*, a show he was publicizing that had won the Tony Award.

When I arrived at the Athletic Club and took the elevator to the dining room, Bill sat waiting for me. After warm hugs, we settled down for breakfast. I noticed how tired he looked, and how much he had aged since I had last seen him in Palm Beach when he was there on business. He slurred some words, but he was cold sober. Then he told me that he'd had a stroke, and it affected his speech. Poor, dear, Bill—how ironic. He sounded drunk even when sober.

I read the rest of the article. He died of cancer, but the story didn't mention what part of his body had been affected. It could have been his lungs. In all the years I had known him, he had been a chain smoker.

I sat there holding the article, remembering all the loving things he surprised me with: There was the Don the Beachcombers dinner in the hospital; a bowl of caviar to relish while he painted my toenails; the limo instead of our usual cab ride to "21" for my birthday. Then there was that memorable Thanksgiving weekend two years after Jonathan and I had left New York. He had phoned and asked, "How about the three of us having Thanksgiving dinner together?" We celebrated at Chesler's Restaurant on Worth Avenue. I noticed how well he looked then, and he was sober.

I loved that man.

# Chapter Twenty

Since his first job as a DJ in Tallahassee shortly after high school, Jonathan moved around. That seemed to be the way it was with DJs. A better job offer and a new city.

I answered the phone one day, and it was Jonathan, calling from a radio station in Des Moines, Iowa. "Mom, I've been dating a girl. We're in love, and we're getting married. Her parents want to meet you. You'll be hearing from them."

After we hung up, I thought about my son. Here he was twenty-four years old and going to become a husband. Where had the time gone?

It wasn't long before my future daughter-in-law's parents in Vero Beach contacted me. We set a date, and they drove the four hours to see me. They were a warm, friendly couple, and we hit it off immediately.

After they arrived and we had a chance to get to know each other, the mother asked, "Caren, why are you staying here, all alone in this town, why don't you move to Vero Beach? We'll help you find an apartment, and you can start giving dancing lessons there. At least you'll be with family."

I gave it some serious thought. Give up my students? Start all over again? It was true. I had no one there I cared about.

I gave up my apartment, turned the studio over to one of my students, and moved back to the coast where I could see the "real" ocean again. I'd had enough of the bay. The new in-laws found a cozy little apartment for me only a few blocks from the beach. It didn't take me long to locate a dance studio, and make arrangements with the dance instructor to rent it twice a week. My classes included Hawaiian, belly dancing, and Disco. Word soon got around, and I started my classes.

One of my students told me her country club was having a big soiree, and asked if I would entertain by belly dancing. She offered a nice fee, and I accepted. I was also hired to dance at private parties, but I wouldn't dance in a public place where the customers put money into the dancer's bra or hip belt. I wanted belly dancing to retain its authenticity as a Middle-Eastern art form and not take on the trappings of a burlesque show.

I began driving to Fort Lauderdale again on weekends to be with Dorothy and teach my former students. The drive to Vero Beach was only an hour and a half longer than Palm Beach was. We went out dancing in the evenings, and professional dancers and instructors often complimented me on my ballroom dancing. I knew I was good, but it was always nice to hear it from the pros.

Back in Vero Beach, I offered to teach ballroom dancing at the Community Center. My first class started at seven o'clock on a Monday evening. About twenty-five people arrived. Over the next several years, that number increased to nearly a hundred. Along with the ballroom dancing, I later added belly dancing and my series of exercises that I renamed "Funtastic Exercises."

The Sheraton Regency Resort Hotel called me about a weekend getaway seminar for women. They wanted to include my Middle-Eastern dancing along with their other events. I agreed to teach these women on a Friday morning. Some who said they just wanted to watch were soon shaking their hips and moving around the floor. When we finished over an hour later, they didn't want it to end. They loved it. So did I.

Vero Beach held its Junior Miss program, which included scholarships for high-school senior girls, and they asked me to be one of the seven judges. Earlier, I had been asked by the family of one of the girls to teach her a dance for the contest. Although she wasn't a dancer, in a few private lessons I taught her a disco routine that rocked the Riverside Theater. She won the contest and received a standing ovation. I was very proud of her, and pleased that I had choreographed the dance number that put her over the top.

A new twist developed in my life when a friend in Palm Beach called. She sold the Cambridge Diet Drink in a multilevel business and wanted to know if I'd be interested in starting the business in Vero Beach.

I told her, "No, sorry, but I'm not interested. I'm busy teaching dancing and don't really have time for anything else."

We left it at that, but soon after, I received a can of the chocolate powder from her. I tried it for myself. It was delicious, so I signed up. I drank it for breakfast every morning. Then my students tried it—and my friends. I soon had people wanting to sign up to sell it like I was doing. So I added another business to my life. I held meetings, wrote newsletters, and after a few months, had to hire a secretary to help me out. I was making good money.

A short time later I was off to Memphis for a leadership training seminar at the Peabody Hotel. It lasted four days, followed by a banquet. A couple of years after that, I flew to Hawaii for their first convention.

By that time, Cambridge took so much of my time that I had to slow down my classes. But I felt it was worth it—I felt better and looked better than ever. And the income was too good to turn down.

Not long after that, I was glad I hadn't given up on my dancing classes because I received a letter in the mail saying that Cambridge had filed for Chapter 11. That was the end of that. I continued with the drink since I had many cans of chocolate drink powder left, and money in the bank.

So I joyfully danced again at parties doing my Middle-Eastern number with veils and cymbals, or the hula in my sarong or grass skirt. I enjoyed a busy life filled with dinner dates and social activities.

It wasn't long before I received that phone call in 1985, I knew I would get some day, since my son had been married five years.

"Mom," Jonathan said, "you're going to be a grandmother."

A grandmother. Well, waddya know? A dancing grandmother.

"When, Jonathan?" I asked.

"Sometime around September."

Jonathan a father? Where had the time gone? So many life changes. He now performed stand-up comedy in clubs around the country in addition to radio. The comedy routine didn't surprise me. His teacher used to tell me he would break them up with his jokes. He had me laughing for years.

I told my friends and students I was expecting a grandchild. Several told me, "Maybe it will be a girl, and you can teach her how to dance." But when the time came, Jonathan called to tell me, "You have a grandson, Mom. We named him Brandon."

I lived in a beautiful townhouse close to the beach where I could hear the breakers in my bedroom at night. I had moved from my small apartment when I sold Cambridge diet drink and needed more room. I'd often walk on the beach with a friend in the early mornings. I liked my comfortable life.

Then I heard from Jonathan that they were leaving for California to try his luck in television. They had an apartment waiting for them, and they were driving their car out to the west coast. As we talked about California, I became lonely for my hometown. It had now been nineteen years since I had driven with Jonathan out of New York in a blizzard. On that drive, I had no idea what lay ahead for us.

I thought of the time I had spent in Florida, what I had accomplished, and the experiences I'd had. There were the dancing lessons, of course, then selling mutual funds and real estate. My short marriage, of course. The trip to Cape Canaveral on the back of a friend's Gold Wing Honda to watch the NASA shuttle *Columbia* blast off. Then more dancing, with Jonathan growing up all the time, and moving on with his life. Now I was a grandmother.

What next?

I phoned Dorothy. "Have you any desire to return to California? Jonathan is moving there, and your sons live there. I think I'd like to go back—how about you?"

Dorothy simply replied, "When do we leave?"

# Chapter Twenty-One

"California here we come—right back where we started from." The words to that old song ran through my head as I packed my car and waited for Dorothy to arrive from Fort Lauderdale with her car and belongings to begin our trip west. We would leave from Vero Beach. The moving van would travel west with our furniture. I had already said my goodbyes to neighbors and friends.

My students said, "We'll miss you and the lessons, Caren."

We headed for Carlsbad, California, a quaint little beach town north of San Diego. Close friends had found us an apartment that we would share only two blocks from the ocean. The weather promised to be nice, and we decided to take our time. I led, Dorothy followed, and we used our newly purchased walkie-talkies, but soon discovered that all we could hear was static. We managed to communicate with hand signals and our turn indicators whenever we wanted to make a rest stop.

After five days and a beautiful trip, we arrived in the pretty little town of Carlsbad. It would only be an hour and a half drive to see our children. After settling into our apartment, we went to the local senior center and asked if they'd be interested in dancing and drama classes . . . and they were. So the following week, I started a class in ballroom and line dancing. Dorothy started a creative drama class, and we joined a Toastmasters club and regularly attended their meetings. We were two busy sixty-something sisters, doing what we liked to do, and close to the ocean we had enjoyed so much when we were kids.

The time passed quickly, and after one year, we were still happily ensconced in Carlsbad. I also taught at the Joslyn Senior Center in Escondido, several miles away. My line dancing classes had been going over big at the mobile home parks. I also had ballroom classes for officers and their wives at the Camp Pendleton Marine Base in nearby Oceanside.

These young Marines and their wives were anxious to learn the foxtrot and "swing." I was happy to see how much they were enjoying these evening classes. I felt it a great honor and privilege when they invited me to be their guest at a black-tie dinner dance to celebrate the 212th anniversary of the United States Marine Corps.

The affair was very impressive. When the Marines marched into the huge room carrying our flag with the music playing "The Marines' Hymn," everyone stood. I glanced around at the wives. They were so young. Their lives seemed peaceful now. The Vietnam and Korean wars were behind us but they'd always be facing the fact that something would erupt again to tear their families apart. I was thankful that we weren't in a war now. I'd seen enough of these brave couples torn apart in WWII some forty years earlier.

On this evening, we didn't know that the Gulf war and Iraq were yet to come. When the seven-week dance classes ended, I was thanked and received many hugs. Then the class handed me a note of appreciation for putting the "swing" and a dose of therapy into their lives.

I remember mother telling me that after WWI—which, supposedly was the war to end all wars—she and Daddy felt the time was right to have a child who would never experience such a conflict. Little did they know that those in my generation would live through more than any other generation.

One evening over dinner, Dorothy and I discussed taking some time off. I asked her, "Do you think it would be possible to get a week in Palm Springs with your time share on such short notice? We've been working hard this past year, and I think we deserve a little vacation. What about you?"

"Great idea," she said. "I'll phone right now."

What luck. A time share was available and waiting for us. Three days later and we were on our way to Palm Springs—wonderful Palm Springs. I had not forgotten that the desert had given me back my normal breathing when I was a child. It felt good to return to that warm climate and such a feeling of peace there.

Once we arrived and inhaled the desert air, we talked about moving from Carlsbad to Palm Springs. We'd miss the ocean, but not the fog. We found a rental complex where we would each have our own apartment; we were always so used to having our own space. We would still be close, however, since these apartments were right across from each other. With that settled, we made the move.

Now that we lived in Palm Springs, we began to make friends. One of my neighbors suggested that I contact a local radio personality who interviewed interesting people. She thought my background would make for a good program. "Tell her you're my friend," she added.

So I called the station and spoke to the lady. We set a morning date.

When I arrived, I was met by a stunning looking blonde who I thought should be on TV instead of hidden behind a radio mike. She taped the interview to be heard at a later date. Before I left, she suggested that I call the society editor of the local paper, *The Desert*

*Sun.* "Tell her I told you to contact her," she said. "I think she'd be interested in writing about you."

I called, and we made a date to meet at a little café in the mall. We had a nice rapport and felt very much at ease with each other. During the interview, when I mentioned I had been Judy Garland's stand-in in *The Wizard of Oz*, she bubbled.

"Caren, this is the fiftieth anniversary of *The Wizard of Oz*. What luck to have you here. I'll suggest to my editor that we do a big story on you. The timing is perfect."

We set a date. I wasn't even aware it had been fifty years since that movie had been made. So much had happened in my life since then. A photographer came to my apartment, and I posed with a copy of the red shoes I wore for the film.

On August 15, 1989, on the front page of the Living section, there I was in living color, and a story that took up most of the page.

I soon became known in the desert for teaching ballroom, tap, Hawaiian, line dancing and Funtastic exercises at country clubs, tennis clubs, resorts, retirement homes, senior centers, the Elderhostel, the Elks Club, the Village Center for the Arts, and parties. I also gave private ballroom and belly dance lessons. The Rancho Mirage Women's Club hired me to teach guests Hawaiian dancing at their luau. They asked me back the following year to teach country-western dancing for their hoedown.

By word of mouth I built a following. My Joslyn Senior Center dancers in Palm Desert performed their western line dancing in various places, including the fourth annual Indian Heritage Festival.

I was even asked to model clothes at a fundraiser for the children's museum. I joined the Desert Swing Dance Club where some of the best dancers in the desert were members. What a pure joy to spend afternoons dancing with men who really danced well.

Another club I eagerly joined was the Variety Club for Children's Charities, with chapters all over the world. The money they raised went to the children's charities in the desert. After several months of being a member, I offered to teach line dancing to the men and women who wanted to perform at the Fourth Annual Cabaret Luncheon to be held at Marriott's Rancho Las Palmas Resort. Twelve members volunteered, and we rehearsed two evenings a week. Though they were not professionals, it was a most commendable performance.

I had heard that Kirk Douglas was having a book signing for his new novel, *The Gift*. I arrived with one of the photos we'd had taken together at Paramount Studios. After purchasing his book I waited patiently in a long line for his autograph. There was a lady seated beside him and as each person approached she would ask their name and pass it on to Kirk, along with their book, to save time.

My turn came as Kirk finished signing for the woman ahead of me. Before his assistant could reach for my book or ask my name, I placed my photo of Kirk and me next to my book. He looked a bit puzzled at the photo in front of him. Then he looked up at me with a big smile and asked, "How've ya been?" Then he signed his novel: To Caren, with fond memories. Kirk Douglas. The line waited while our picture was taken.

I headed home with the photo and book tucked in my bag and a good feeling tucked in my heart. This world famous mega movie star hadn't changed. He was the same nice guy I'd met at Paramount Studios over forty years earlier. We didn't know then that Kirk would survive a helicopter crash and later a stroke.

Jonathan also kept busy and soon booked Palm Springs for his stand-up comedy routine at a club called "The Laff Stop." It was his third engagement in the desert. He had previously been doing comedy all over the country along with his career in radio. I was always proud of the fact that audiences enjoyed him and his routines even though he never used four-letter words.

After seven years, Jonathan's marriage had come to an end. My grandson, Brandon, moved to Florida with his mother.

A year later, Jonathan met Lori St. James when they both attended an acting school in North Hollywood. Lori was a singer as well as an actress. I had the opportunity to meet her when Jonathan took me to the Queen Mary in Long Beach one evening to hear her perform with two other girls. Lori had a beautiful voice and was a stunning looking young lady. I was glad they were happy together and delighted when, three years later, they got married.

Brandon soon became a "frequent flyer" because of his many visits to be with his dad and Lori. It also gave us the opportunity to be together often enough so I could watch him grow and develop as he entered his teens. He was becoming a fine young man, like his dad.

For two years, I taught western line dancing every Tuesday evening in the lounge of the Gene Autry Resort Hotel. Some of the patrons who joined the class were well-known entertainers. The walls were lined with framed pictures of movie stars. I was surprised to find a photo of me with Roy Rogers that had been taken on a movie set years ago. When one of the group noticed the photo, she took a picture of me beside it.

The entertainment columnist, Frederick Heider, of our Palm Springs paper, watched from one of the nearby tables. Two days later, he mentioned in his column that people should drop in and join my class.

When his column came out, I phoned to thank him for the plug. Then he said, "I understand that you teach ballroom dancing. The West Coast Opera Company is putting on the Harvest Moon Ball in my honor. It's a fundraiser to be held at the Autry Resort." Then he asked, "Do you know Lou De Grado?"

"No, I don't."

"He's an excellent dancer, and I think you'd make a good team to demonstrate the dances. Would you be interested?"

"Yes, of course I would."

"Then I'd like you to join us at our next meeting where we're planning the event."

"Thanks, I'll be glad to."

At the meeting, they introduced me to my future dance partner. We were a perfect height for each other. Lou was good-looking with an engaging personality, and I liked him immediately. We met for several rehearsals in preparation for the event. I felt lucky to have him for a partner and friend.

The night of the ball, a sixteen-piece orchestra played. There was dinner, dancing, and then the contest. Lou and I were to give a one-minute demonstration of each of the six dances that the contestants would be asked to do: the fox trot, waltz, swing, cha-cha, polka, and the country two-step. After our first one-minute demonstration, the contestants poured out onto the floor for the fox trot. The same was repeated for the other five dances.

The judges were Alice Faye, Jane Withers, Ruta Lee, and Donald O'Connor. The grand prize was a fifteen-day cruise through the Panama Canal for two, on the *Star Odyssey*. The profits for the evening benefited the West Coast Opera company.

When the contest was over, Lou and I danced the remainder of the evening. He was a fun partner, with a way of expressing such freedom and joy that he seemed to be in another world, and took me there with him. I knew we would be dancing professionally and socially from then on. The next few years we performed at many different events from jitterbugging at a '40s party in the Palm Spring's Air Museum to line dancing for a hoedown fund-raiser for AIDS.

Another dance contest. This one held at the Indian-owned Fantasy Springs Casino in Indio, about twenty miles east of Palm

Springs. They asked me to be one of two judges. Even before the contest started, the floor filled with dancers swinging to the Big Band sound of Ted Herman's orchestra. One look at the contestants, and I realized it was going to be tough to pick a winner.

I noticed a young couple who looked to be in their twenties. He wore a World War II army uniform. She looked as though she had just stepped out of the '40s. The sight of them took me back to my nights at the Hollywood Canteen. I had to know more about that couple.

When the music stopped, I followed them to their table.

"Hi," I said. "You look fabulous. How come you're dressed up like the war years?"

He introduced me to his partner, and told me he was Josh Curtis. He explained he was enamored with anything that had to do with the 1940s. He said all his clothes were vintage 1940s, and so were his cars. He had collected memorabilia from movies of that period and planned to open a museum sometime in the future. I recognized his name as a well-known artist and photographer in the desert who was called "That Forties Guy."

Ted Herman announced that the contest was about to begin. Minutes later, good dancers covered the ballroom floor. A middle-aged couple, who did a mean jitterbug, won the contest. But Josh and his partner won my heart.

# Chapter Twenty-Two

One day I received a copy of the *Los Angeles Times*, dated August 2, 1999, from a reporter on the newspaper. In it was a story about the July 12, 1949, Chatsworth plane crash. I was in two of the photos.

The reporter had phoned me a month before and told me she would be writing about the fiftieth anniversary of the crash that I had survived. She had tracked me down along with several other survivors and wanted to do a phone interview.

I asked her why a story on this particular crash, since there had been others in the past fifty years.

"This was the worst one in Southern California," she replied.

During the interview, she impressed me as being a very good reporter. When we were finished, she said, "I want to send our photographer out to Palm Springs to shoot some pictures of you on Monday—is that all right?"

"I'm sorry," I said, "but that's the day I volunteer for the Stroke Activity Center."

She understood and told me, "That's okay, Caren. We'll send the photographer to the Stroke Activity Center and shoot the pictures there."

When he arrived on Monday, he handed me a copy of the 1949

paper with the dreadful headlines: "35 Die as L.A. Plane Rams Into Mountains."

"Now, Caren," he said, lining up for a shot, "stand over there and hold the paper so the headline faces the camera. Now look up, with a faraway expression, as if you're remembering that terrible day."

I did as he suggested, but I wasn't pretending as I recalled the horrors of that day and gave thanks that I survived.

After the photo session, it was time for me to be with my people at the Center. He asked, "How often do you come here?"

"Twice a month."

"And how long have you been volunteering?"

"Since I came to the desert in 1989."

He asked if he could take a few shots showing what I did. We entered a room known as the Paul Newman Rehabilitation Theater where my "clients" greeted me. I put a tape in my boom box, and the music started. Everyone moved to the music however best they could, whether seated, or standing up holding my hands for support. Some could only move a hand or an arm. Others managed to get on their feet. It was always an inspiring sight to see their faces light up.

I always told them, "You don't have to do steps, just listen to the music, and move whatever part of your body you can."

Established in 1978, the Palm Springs Stroke Activity Center (now the Stroke Recovery Center) offers a day facility for stroke survivors who receive psychological, physical, and speech therapies free of charge five days a week.

Their fall fund-raiser, the Wonderland Ball, is a glamorous evening in a beautiful hotel setting. Lou and I always look forward to the evening and dancing to the music of a well-known orchestra.

Another activity I thoroughly enjoyed was the Toastmasters that offered several different desert branches. I had given an eight-minute speech at one of our meetings on "Smashing the Stereotypes of the Senior Citizen." One of my fellow Toastmasters said to me afterwards, "Caren, that speech you just gave is so good, you should enter the Toastmaster's Competition." I would be representing the Palm Springs club. Since this speech was about staying young, I decided it was time to come out of the closet and admit my age—seventy-one.

I entered the competition and won. I also competed against the winners from clubs all over Riverside County. Again, I won another trophy. Hawaii hosted the semifinals. Winners, who participated there, arrived from all over the country. We weren't permitted to repeat the same speech, so I decided to talk about my near-death experience in the plane crash.

The night of the big event, I walked on stage and gave my speech. Although I didn't win, the applause acknowledged me warmly. What a memorable experience, and the thrill of being there had been worth the trip.

Dorothy and I were invited again to the famous Jivin' Jacks and Jills fifteenth annual Hollywood reunion, held in the Empire Room of The Sportsmen's Lodge, in Studio City. Michael Fitzgerald and Gary Bell sponsored the event with a Sunday luncheon. Many of our fellow entertainers attended—a chance to see some of those we might never see if not for that reunion.

During the luncheon, a gentleman approached me. "Hi," he said, "we worked together in *Best Foot Forward* years ago." I thought, my gawd, he recognized me after fifty-three years. "It's sure good to see you again," he said. The music began to play, he said, "Let's dance." We moved onto the floor and started swinging. Where had the years gone?

After lunch, they showed film clips of those in attendance on a large screen. They included one of my scenes from *The Navajo Kid*, and another clip of my sister Dorothy in a scene from *Cry Havoc*.

Peggy Ryan, well remembered for her dancing with Donald

O'Connor in musicals, furnished the afternoon entertainment. She had flown in from Las Vegas with her dance troupe of beautiful women. Ever the bubbly and adorable lady, she and her troupe put on a good show.

Ann Rutherford, who played Polly Benedict in the *Andy Hardy* movies and Scarlett's sister in *Gone With the Wind*, attended too, and we recalled the double-dates we went on when both in our teens.

We exchanged warm hugs with Marsha Hunt, Jane Withers, and Jacqueline White, who flew in from Houston to be there.

Autograph hunters waited in the lobby to gather celebrity signatures. It was an event we looked forward to every year.

Dorothy came over one day looking quite pleased about something. She brought a video tape with her. There was no name on the cover, and when I asked what it was about, she smiled. I thought maybe it was a tape of one of the movies she had appeared in years ago. I slipped it into the VCR.

The screen lit up, but there was no title or names popping up. The first scene made its appearance with a couple of soldiers conversing. The next scene looked like the interior of a train station. Then a long shot of a girl entering. Was that Dorothy, I wondered? The girl carried a suitcase as she walked across the floor to the ticket counter. Somehow she looked familiar. Then a closer shot. I stared at the screen in disbelief. "Oh my God," I yelled, "that's me!"

It was a scene from that Army training film, *Pickup Girl*, I made at Paramount over fifty years ago. I couldn't believe it—finally I would get to see the end of the picture.

"Dorothy," I asked, somewhat bewildered, "where in the world did you get this film? I didn't think I'd ever see it again." I was genuinely surprised and delighted, and I asked her again, "How did you ever get your hands on this?"

She told me that Michael Fitzgerald, who sponsored the Jivin'

Jacks and Jills luncheon, sent it to her. He wanted Dorothy to surprise me with it. Michael had gotten it from a friend in Memphis, Mitch Schaperkotter, one of the founders of the Memphis Film Festival, who had discovered the film years after World War II. It seemed Mitch had recognized me as the same girl he had seen in *The Navajo Kid* and knew Michael would get it to me somehow. Michael then enlisted Dorothy to deliver the goods.

Thanks to the movies *The Navajo Kid* and *Hands Across the Border*, the organizers of the Memphis Western Film Festival of 1999, invited me to be a celebrity guest. This was my first time at any festival, and I was thrilled. Thirteen other celebrities also attended the three-day festival.

They screened five of the films I had appeared in: *The Navajo Kid*, *Hands Across the Border*, *Wild Harvest*, *My Best Gal*, and the Army film, *Pickup Girl*. After each screening, each of us said a few words and answered questions from the audience.

We displayed our photos on long tables in the hotel ballroom. Boyd Magers and his wife Donna shared a table with me. Boyd, the editor/publisher of *Western Clippings*, also owned and operated Video West, Inc. He had written four books, and it was a treat to be with them.

Hundreds of people looked over the photos, talked to the celebrities, and selected pictures they wanted us to autograph. Some wanted to pose with us for photos. I was surprised at how many people recognized me after all those years.

Dealers sold rare Western memorabilia on some tables. One dealer across from me left his table and walked over and handed me a little box. Inside was a tiny gold western saddle, studded in rhinestones, dangling from a gold chain. "This is for you," he said.

I thanked him and asked, "Why are you giving me such a nice present?"

"I'd just like you to have it," he said with a big smile.

Later, another dealer came over to me. "I hear you were Judy Garland's stand-in, in *The Wizard of Oz*." He handed me a rare post-card of Judy and added, "I thought maybe you'd like to have this."

I met so many warm and friendly people.

The following day, I was to be seated with three other actors and board member Ray Nielson at a long table on a dais high above the audience. Each of us had a mike so we could answer questions about our careers.

There was just one problem. As I sat down, I couldn't see the whole audience over the table. I heard a few giggles as I sat there. I stretched as high as I could, but it became obvious I needed help. Someone suggested a couple of telephone books. I told the actor next to me, "If they bring me a high chair, I'm outta here."

A gentleman brought out another one of those stack chairs and that solved the problem. We held a Q & A session for several hours.

It was three wonderful days, and I enjoyed every one. Early each morning I rushed down to the hotel dining room to devour one of those great southern buffet breakfasts of bacon, sausage, eggs, fried potatoes, grits, and hot biscuits.

One morning I overheard two celebrities at the next table talking. One of them asked the other, "How does such a little thing like her pack away all that food?"

It didn't bother me—I knew when I got home, I'd dance it off.

The last night during the beautiful banquet, we each received a plaque. Mine featured a picture of Bob Steele and me in *The Navajo Kid* and was engraved with:

Memphis Film Festival
Special Guest
Caren Marsh
1999

Ray and Sharon Court hold their Hollywood Collectors and Celebrities show in North Hollywood four times a year. I had heard about this show and was invited to attend.

They filled their ballroom with long tables, much like it had been in Memphis. Again, we sat at tables with our photos spread out before us. Some of us weren't big names, others were well known, and some would be considered stars.

Along with my photos, I had on display a stack of books, *Bob Steele and His Reel Women*. Previously, I had received a letter from the author, Bob Nareau, telling me he wrote this book. Since I had been one of Bob Steele's leading ladies, he wanted me to send him a photo of myself in a western costume to be included in the book. He asked me to write the preface, and I was thrilled to oblige. Later, when I received a copy of the book, much to my surprise, he put my picture on the cover.

A gentleman approached my table, looked over my assortment of photos, picked up one in a western costume, and asked, "Do you have any more of these?"

"Yes, I do."

"Fine," he said, "I'll take a dozen of them. And don't autograph them to me, just sign your name."

I did as he requested, then wondered what he was going to do with them. Later, I learned that some dealers and collectors buy them from celebrities, then sell them to fans for a profit.

I looked over the crowd and saw Johnny Grant, honorary Mayor of Hollywood. He strolled up and down the aisles and visited everyone. I caught up with him, introduced myself, and told him I had heard him speak at our Hollywood High School reunion the previous year. He remembered and greeted me with a warm smile. To me, he'll always be the perfect mayor for my hometown.

# Chapter Twenty-Three

The phone rang. Miss Jean Nelson said she was calling from Chesterton, Indiana. My first thought was, I don't know anyone in Chesterton, wherever that is; in fact, I don't know anyone in Indiana.

As the founder of *The Wizard of Oz* Festival there, she told me the nineteenth annual meeting would be held September 15 through the 17, 2000. She immediately had my attention. Jean had discovered that I was Judy's stand-in and wanted me to be their guest for a three-day weekend—expenses paid—and I could bring a companion. She asked me to bring some photos to autograph. "They come here from all over the country," she said.

"Will the Munchkins be there?" I asked.

"Of course," she added, "and you will all ride in the parade."

Ride in a parade? I would finally get to ride in a parade after my disappointment back in 1939 at the Rose Bowl Parade. How about that!

Jean went on to say, "You'll have an Ambassador to look after you for the three days of your visit."

I quickly accepted the invitation.

A few weeks later, the organizers of the Iverson Movie Ranch Wild, Wild West Festival in Chatsworth, California, invited me to participate. It was scheduled for the same weekend as the *Wizard of*

*Oz* Festival. They had planned to add my hand and boot prints in cement in the courtyard along with other Western actors. Bob Steele and I had filmed *The Navajo Kid* there, and later that's where the airplane I was in slammed into the mountain.

I had to decline the Wild West Festival but was delighted when they invited me to attend the following year, which I did.

When I left for Indiana, Dorothy flew with me. We were off to see the Munchkins—the wonderful Munchkins of Oz. Arriving at O'Hare International Airport in Chicago around midnight, we were greeted by a very patient couple who drove us to Chesterton, two hours away.

We had very little sleep, and then later that day, we all met at Jean Nelson's Yellow Brick Road Gift Shop and Fantasy Museum for lunch. The gift shop carried all manner of wizardly items, including every size of ruby red slippers imaginable. I never dreamed that sixty-two years would go by before I'd have the opportunity to see some of the little Munchkins again.

An ambassador had been assigned to us. She had the responsibility of seeing that we got to the autograph stations, lunches, dinners, and take in whatever sights we wanted. She offered to drive us around Chesterton to satisfy our curiosity about the town. We saw beautiful homes with lots of green space, manicured gardens and lawns, and no fences in sight. The center of town with all the little stores and shops seemed like cruising the back lot at MGM.

Our Ambassador told us, "I thought you'd like to see the main street as it is now. When the festival starts tomorrow, they'll be jammed with booths of all kinds, and no cars will be allowed to drive through here."

The next day at one of the autograph sessions, I shared a table with the Munchkins. Adults and children filed by with their *Oz* treasures for us to sign. Others lined up to hand us their dolls, books, cards, figurines, posters, T-shirts, cups and . . . you name it, they had it. I couldn't believe how many different kinds of memorabilia were on the market.

I signed photos I had spread out on the table. Some wanted their pictures taken with me. There were so many little well-behaved children, who had probably been to the festival before. They knew that in some way I had something to do with Dorothy in the *Wizard of Oz*—a movie they probably had seen dozens of times on TV.

Two good-looking young men, William Stillman and Jay Scarfone, authors of many *Oz* books, including their famous fiftieth anniversary edition of *The Wizard of Oz*, were there selling their books. I'd never seen anything like the one with the pop-up images—it was incredible. I had to have it when I saw the *Oz* story pop right out of the pages—it was so cleverly done.

On the morning of the parade, I sat in the front seat of a Mercedes convertible driven by an attractive young lady. On each side of the car was a huge sign:

CAREN MARSH - DOLL
ACTRESS
JUDY GARLAND'S STAND-IN

I smiled and waved to the crowds. They smiled and waved back, making up for my disappointment at not having been in the Rose Bowl Parade many years ago. It was as if the good witch, Glinda, had waved her magic wand back then and said, "Don't feel bad, Caren, sixty-two years from now you will ride in the *Wizard of Oz* Parade."

Dorothys were everywhere. Toddlers, teenagers, young women and mature women, all dressed like Dorothy in the movie. Some carried baskets with stuffed dogs inside peeking out. All wore sparkling ruby red slippers. I even saw several Tin Woodsmen and Scarecrows. I couldn't believe it when I saw a dog dressed as Dorothy.

Everywhere the magic of Oz, and the spirit of L. Frank Baum, who wrote the famous book, brought all this to life. I bet that MGM never dreamed their film would result in such adulation so many years later.

As for me, I couldn't have imagined I'd be in the center of all this wizardly devotion to such wonderful fantasy. And to Jean Nelson, I give credit for visualizing and organizing the Oz festival that had drawn thousands of people to be a part of it.

On the last day, our ambassador drove us to the "Munchkin breakfast." They sat me at a long table with the Munchkins. Lines of people filed past and requested our autographs before being seated at their tables.

At the end of the day everyone followed the Munchkins as we walked to Centennial Park. They gathered around the bandstand where we stood on a dais high up above the crowds for the Grand Finale. The song "We're off to see the Wizard" floated through the air. We were there to say goodbye. Townspeople dressed as characters from the movie, along with the Munchkins and myself, stepped forward, one at a time to say a few words. As I stood there and looked down at the crowd, some of the people wiped their eyes. Others stood and waved. The impact this movie has had on people's hearts overwhelmed me. They all love *The Wizard of Oz*. Then over the loudspeaker, we heard Judy's voice, singing "Over the Rainbow" as the crowd joined in.

The festival ended on a sentimental note with cries of "See you next year" that rang in the air. It was as if we had all been transported to another time, another place.

When the 34th annual Munchkin Convention was held in Harrisburg, PA., I was invited to attend. This festival focused on the Oz collector. It was a weekend that included costume contests and memorabilia of all kinds from dealers around the country. Signing

my photos and meeting all the festival fans kept me busy and I enjoyed every bit of it.

On Saturday night, William "Bill" Stillman, co-author of many
famous *Oz* books, interviewed me on stage. Many questions about
Judy and the movie were asked afterwards by the audience.

On our last day, Bill drove me to his and Jay's home for a TV
interview he'd arranged for me. From the time I stepped into
their house I was surrounded by all their *Oz* treasures. Upstairs I
was greeted by life-size figures of Dorothy, the Scarecrow, the Tin
Woodsman, and the Cowardly Lion. They were standing together in
a corner of the room and looked very much alive. In another corner
was a flying monkey, so lifelike that if I'd been dressed as Dorothy I
thought he'd surely have carried me off.

This was another amazing *Oz* weekend and I had a marvelous
time.

Then another festival and another invitation to be a celebrity
guest. This one was in Kansas. The town of Liberal was famous for
their "Dorothy House." I couldn't wait to see it. To my surprise the
interior had scenes from the movie done so magnificently that it
took my breath away. Everyone who loves *The Wizard of Oz* would
be amazed by what I saw. There were lifelike scenes showing everything from the Scarecrow in the field to the talking trees and the
Emerald City. These were not simply pictures; they were actual set-
tings with life-size figures. What an awesome display.

The day of the parade was so cold and windy that we couldn't be
outside. The Munchkins and I rode in a warm limousine with the
windows lowered just enough to enable us to stick our hands out and
wave to the bystanders who were bundled up on the curb.

I felt a bit of nostalgia being in Kansas and recalling those days
on the MGM set that seemed so real. But that was Hollywood,
where they could build a set that could place you anywhere at any

time, and make you believe it. But this was the real Kansas and I was having a taste of it.

On the airplane heading home once more, I sat back, relaxed, and thought about previous festivals. I'd been invited more than once to most of them and had the honor of being the Grand Marshal in the parade one year in Chesterton, Indiana.

Sudden turbulence interrupted my thoughts. The plane shook violently and jostled me from side to side in spite of my secured seat belt. Each frightening bump or jolt triggered the memory of my plane crash, the miracle of my survival, and the doctors who told me I'd never dance again.

When the flight smoothed out, I felt an inner calm even though the last few moments had been distressing. Leaning back in my seat, I focused on my students who would be waiting for me in tomorrow's class. I thought about all the various dances I had learned and taught over the years: ballet, tap, Spanish, Hawaiian, Tahitian, ballroom, belly dancing, country western and line dancing. They were all-important influences in my life.

As we approached Palm Springs, other memories returned as I looked out over the beautiful homes, swimming pools, golf courses and country clubs with man-made lakes and paved streets. I recalled my first trip to Palm Springs with my family when we drove along a dirt road in the middle of the night to reach "The Village."

We landed safely at the airport and I took a cab home past apartment houses, condos, restaurants, shopping centers and a movie complex with ten theatres. I saw a huge lighted sign in front of the Indian-owned Spa Resort Casino where seventy-six years ago a small wooden structure stood where Mother, Dorothy and I took the mineral baths from the Indian ladies.

Daddy's words came back to me from long ago when Mr. Cable told him he could buy an acre of land for two hundred dollars. "Now what would I do with an acre of sand in a barren desert?" he replied.

Yes, through the years there has been growth and changes in Palm Springs as well as my hometown, Hollywood. For example, if you were standing on the corner of Hollywood Boulevard and Highland Avenue where the legendary Hollywood Hotel once stood, you would see the recently developed shopping mecca that includes the impressive Kodak Theatre. In 2002 this became the new home of the Academy Awards ceremony. On the corner of Hollywood and Vine, the Dyas Department Store stood before becoming the Broadway Hollywood. We had bought our clothes there, Christmas shopped there, and throughout my childhood I considered it to be my store. I remember that beautiful red gown with the red ostrich feathers that I couldn't have for my sixteenth birthday. Now I'm told that offices have replaced my Broadway Hollywood.

The Max Factor makeup studio that was once on Highland Avenue across from Hollywood High School is no longer there. How excited I was when I purchased my first pair of eyelashes there for *A Midsummer Night's Dream* in the Hollywood Bowl. It is now the Hollywood Museum and holds thousands of movie collectables.

My once beautiful one-bedroom apartment at Hollywood Boulevard and Laurel Canyon where I lived for five years held some wonderful memories. I was carried over the threshold as a happy new bride.

Then on December 7, the shocking news of Pearl Harbor —and some drastic changes. We would drape black fabric over our windows at night, and hear the wail of the sirens during air-raid drills. There was food rationing and gas rationing. I have all those memories of the years living in our beautiful, rental apartment. We paid fifty-five dollars a month then. I understand it is now a condo worth over half a million dollars.

The biggest growth and changes, however, have been in *me*; so many challenges that made me stronger; so many experiences that forced me to grow. As I continue down my own yellow brick road, I look forward to more opportunities not knowing what to expect next. Though I never actually met a Scarecrow, a Tin Woodsman or a Cowardly Lion, I did meet many wolves along the way.

I feel an energy and optimism as I head into tomorrow living one day at a time. Best of all I'm finding contentment and peace within that I never dreamed I could have.

Relaxing at sister Dorothy's pool in North Hollywood.

Showing belly
dance movement
to students in Ft.
Lauderdale.

Teaching Hawaiian dancing.

"Carena"

At a belly dancing
convention as
"Carena."

Entertaining at the Flying Farmers Social Event in Sarasota, Florida

Tambil                    Teena

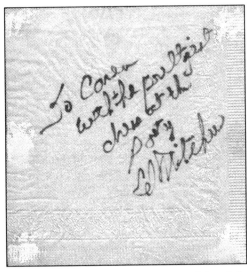

**Napkin signed by astronaut Commander Edger Mitchell.**

THE NEW YORK TIMES, SUNDAY, MARCH 4, 1979

# Bill Doll, Prominent Press Agent

### By PETER B. FLINT

Bill Doll, a leading show-business press agent, died Friday of cancer in Englewood (N.J.) Hospital. He was 68 years old.

The jovial and dynamic Mr. Doll, who insisted on being called a press agent, not a public relations counselor, was a widely known and popular figure in the Broadway theater district for more than 40 years. His down-to-earth charm gained him a reputation of knowing as many amusement reporters and editors as anyone in his business, and he had an extraordinary talent for garnering news space for his clients.

His office was called Bill Doll & Company, the National Press Agents, and his peripatetic and charismatic manners matched the name. He had lived in Manhattan until 1976, when he retired to the Actors' Home in Englewood after suffering a stroke.

### 200 Shows to His Credit

A witty, outgoing raconteur, he publicized more than 200 Broadway shows, circuses and ice shows, including Mike Todd productions for nearly 30 years, and such personalities as Mae West, Gypsy Rose Lee, Judy Garland, Ken Murray, Louis Armstrong, Spike Jones, Jack Benny and Sally Rand. Mr. Doll also helped sell such diverse products as Silly Putty and sporting equipment made by the company headed by Ted Williams, the former baseball star.

To garner attention, Mr. Doll promoted such stunts as a dance by Bill (Bojangles) Robinson 17 blocks down Broadway during the run of "The Hot Mikado," a tea party for Gargantua, checking a bear from the Moscow Circus into a hotel, a wedding in the circus ring and having a monkey as a luncheon guest at Sardi's, the Times Square watering place that Mr. Doll frequented.

### Publicity Came First

In his office hung a large photograph of Mike Todd on which the flamboyant producer had written: "Bill, you made me what I am today, but I still like you." Mr. Doll man had represented the late producer for nearly 30 years, from "The Hot Mikado," his first musical on Broadway, to his movie extravaganza, "Around the World in 80 Days."

Among the productions for which Mr. Doll beat the drums were such diverse fare as "Top Banana," "New Faces of 1952," a world tour of "Porgy and Bess," "The Saint of Bleecker Street," "Anastasia," "The Threepenny Opera," "Waiting for Godot," "Compulsion," "A Taste of Honey" and "Applause."

Films he helped publicize included "Winged Victory," when he was a sergeant in the Army Air Forces in World War II, "La Dolce Vita," "Long Day's Journey Into Night" and "Mondo Cane."

He was also long associated with such attractions as the Ringling Brothers and Barnum & Bailey Circus, the touring Ice Shows and the Jones Beach Marine Theater on Long Island.

Mr. Doll was a graduate of West Virginia University.

Surviving are two sons, William Michael and Jonathan.

A memorial service will be held soon at a date to be set.

Jonathan doing stand-up comedy in a club.

## WIZARD disk jockey among nation's best

JONATHAN DOLL, air personality for radio station WIZD, known as WIZARD 99, has been named one of the top five disc jockeys in the United States. Drake-Chenault, a California-based company that provides radio stations with various services such as syndicated formats and special features named Doll as a winner after conducting a nationwide search and listening to the on-air work of hundreds of on-air personalities. Doll works the afternoon, 2 p.m. to 6 p.m., shift for WIZARD 99.

Jonathan, the radio "Wizard," in Florida, 1980.

Jonathan with singer-actress Lori St. James.

With Grandson Brandon.

Jonathan and Brandon
visiting Palm Springs.

With Toastmasters Award.

Giving a Toastmasters speech.

My picture with
Roy Rogers at
the Gene Autry
Resort.

Rehearsing for the Harvest Moon Ball with Lou De Grado in Palm Springs.

Left to Right: Ann Richards, Ann Rutherford, Dorothy Morris, Me, and Marsha Hunt. Lunch at the home of Josh Curtis.

Josh Curtis in his 1940
Buick.

Kirk Douglas' book
signing in Palm
Springs

With Leonard Maltin at the
Jivin' Jacks and Jills luncheon.

Jivin' Jacks and Jills annual
luncheon. Dancing with Jim
Pilcher whom I hadn't seen
since *Best Foot Forward*,
fifty-three years earlier.

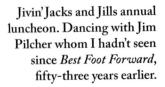

Western actors together at the Memphis Film Festival.
I'm second from right in first row.

Showing a group of festivalgoers how to line dance
at the Judy Garland Festival in Minnesota.

Munchkins and me at Chesterton, Indiana, *Wizard of Oz* Festival.

With *Wizard of Oz* Munchkin Jerry Maren, "The Lollipop Kid," at Chesterton, Indiana, *Wizard of Oz* Festival.

Modeling for children's museum
fundraiser in Palm Springs.

With Munchkin Margaret Pellegrini
at the *Oz* Festival in Kansas.

Flying Monkey in William
Stillmans' *Oz* collection.

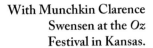

With Munchkin Clarence
Swensen at the *Oz*
Festival in Kansas.

With Joe Luft, Judy's Son,
in Grand Rapids, MN.

Dog dressed as "Dorothy"
at one of the *Wizard
of Oz* Festivals.

The 1940s.

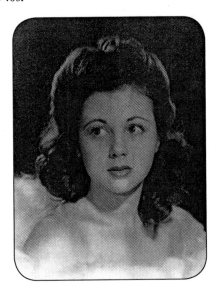

Portrait sketch in pencil and charcoal. "The Sisters" by Josh Curtis, 1997.

1970s

Current day photo.

Breinigsville, PA USA
01 April 2010
235334BV00004B/7/A